First Time Tourists
Malta 2013

From
The Recycled Teenagers Travel Blogs
Aka
First Time Tourists

Suzanne Harvey

To Jacky

Thank you for knowing Mike and me so completely.

This was a gift that took us further from home than our wildest dreams,

Thank you.

CHAPTER 1

Or

How our travels started

During the summer of 2012 we had been thinking of taking a holiday as neither of us has been on one since we were children traveling on our parents' passports.

By holiday I meant one that was not interrupted with having to call work up to 4 times a day whilst away, as in Mike's case, when he had been working for a big national firm. We could not count it as a holiday, more of an extended office break, but that was before we met.

I had been busy working and bringing up my three children with their father, my first husband, and as soon as we had saved for a holiday, we could guarantee a bill or something unexpected would happen.

However, over the years Mike and I got divorced from our respective spouses and eventually we met in 2002. Then recently, because of our ages and certain foibles with our health, we began wondering if a holiday abroad would be workable. A good time to go would be now before we got too old!

Now fate has a wonderful way of knocking you down and then building you up again, and in October 2012 it certainly knocked us sideways. Mike had been passing blood, so it was off to the doctor's for him. They did not hang about; appointments were made with consultants, bloods and samples taken, and then he returned home to wait until all the results came through. During this time he had to claim sick benefits, something he had never done before but I helped him though the form filling as, for obvious reasons, his mind was elsewhere.

Then the results came through on the phone. He had to have a colonoscopy to look for cancer. Two days later he was in hospital and biopsies were also taken.

Another wait for the results.

Finally, 5 days later, with Mike looking worn out and worried, the phone went. It was news of the results. He put it on loud speaker and we both looked at each other as the words, "First let me tell you the good news. It is NOT cancer." We looked at each other, and I could see the pain and worry fading from his face. "So what is it please Dr.?" Mike asked. "Its' Ulcerative Colitis." The Doctor then went on about what to expect and could Mike go in and see him please, but we did not hear any of that, only, "It is NOT cancer."

As soon as the call finished, we both went onto the Internet and researched everything we could about Ulcerative Colitis (UV). The general information was diet, well that was easy as they had diagnosed me with Type 2 Diabetes 2 years previously we already were eating healthily, but with UC fibre is very important.

After a further visit to the doctors, they prescribed Mike some medications. We called it his 'kitty litter' as that is just what it looked like, and in the little aluminum pouch, when you shook it the packet sounded like it too! Mike swore the stuff tasted like kitty litter, too. How he knew that was anyone's guess!

Mike was home from work for about 8 weeks, as he had to wait for the bleeding to stop. Fate has a mysterious way of treating us sometimes. What it takes away with one hand, it gives back with the other. November 2012 turned out to be the wettest for 50 years, raining heavily every day, and soon the Somerset levels were under water. This meant that Mike got to stay in and stay dry without having to stand on his stall in a drafty shopping mall where the wind funneled through right where his stall was, and sometimes, bringing with it the rain.

About early December, Mike was ready to go back to work. Or so he said. He still looked tired to me and somewhat worn with the strain. However, the rent for the stall we had in the shopping mall would not pay for itself, so back he went, on a freezing and blustery day. The wind had not changed, but now we had snow instead of rain.

It had been snowing the day before, and some of it had blown in and around his stand. He had been there for a couple of hours, stamping his feet to keep warm when a friend saw him.

We had not told Jacky about Mike's scare as she had recently lost her own husband to cancer, so when she saw Mike stamping his feet and not looking too well, she asked if he was all right.

"I'm fine." He replied, "Just cannot seem to warm up, especially my feet."

She looked down and giggled.

"I'm not surprised," she said "you are standing in 3 inches of snow… in your slippers!"

He looked down as well and then, the fact he had been there for over three hours, if you count the setting up time too, in 3 inches of snow and had not once thought about what he was wearing on his feet, made him realise just how worried he had been about going back to work.

She kindly watched the stall for him as he went off to buy a nice pair of thick socks and some boots. He had socks on but they were damp and he really did need to warm his feet up fast!

Then as soon as he came back, she dashed off to get him a hot chocolate and a pasty to warm him up from the inside. Trust me when I say that he told me later it was one of the best hot chocolates of his life. He said he could actually feel it coursing through his very veins as he warmed up.

Jacky then left Mike and called me. She asked if everything was all right with him as he did not look at all well. Knowing her husband also had cancer, and she had been a friend for years, I thought it best to tell her the truth. I told her he had gone through all the tests but that it was UC and if he ate a good diet and took his 'kitty litter' he should not have such a bad flare up again.

That's when she told me how she had found him in his slippers and I thanked her for looking after him as I was 40 miles away at home, unwell with a fibromyalgia flare up and could not be there for him.

Jacky asked me when we had last had a holiday and I explained we were hoping to have our first one as adults next year. We hoped that if all went well and Mike could make the money back that we had used whilst he was unwell, we would have enough. He had to continue paying for the shopping mall rent so he did not lose his stall.

Thankfully, it was coming up to Christmas time and there was every chance that he could make the money back, but, after his scare he had given up the stall and get a little shop in Weston, but that would not be until be next year and with a friend that could help him should he be ill again. Jacky agreed that not only would this would be a good idea, but that with him not having to travel so far or get up so early in the morning and stand in all weathers, his health should improve considerably.

She asked if we had anywhere in mind for a holiday and I said that Malta had come up in conversation several times, as Mike had never been there. They speak English and drive on the left-hand side of the road. She said it sounded a wonderful idea due to all the positive points about the language, etc. This could mean Mike would more than likely be able to rest without worrying about how to communicate with local people when shopping and on tours. So much of Malta still has remnants of the days of British rule, yet they have such a different culture we would know we were in different climes and so could thoroughly enjoy ourselves.

Jacky and I finished talking, and she said she had to go, but she would pop in and see me before Christmas to make sure everything was still all right with both of us.

Three days later, there was a knock on the door and Jacky came in. We sat and had a cup of coffee and caught up with each other. When it was time to go, she handed me an envelope and told me to open it when she had left.

I had to admit I was very curious and, putting the kettle back on, sat down and opened the envelope. I was astounded by what was inside. There was the information to go on-line to an account she had set up for us with a company called onthebeach.co.uk. The account contained airline tickets and a hotel room all paid for a week on Malta and enough money to buy insurance and for spending too. Jacky had totally taken me aback at such a generous gift. Flabbergasted just didn't cover it.

I immediately phoned Jackie, well as soon as I knew she would be home and not driving, oh and as soon as I had stopped blubbering too. I thanked her and asked her to explain as this was too great a gift.

"It is not a gift it is something my husband told me to give to you when the time was right, and the time is now. You both need a break and I had promised him I would not give you the cash per se because Mike would spend it on stock and as you support him in everything he does, you would have agreed to it. You both need a holiday as soon as possible, so I thought now would be the right time."

I thanked her again, knowing Mike would call her when he got in and do the same. He did too, because I just couldn't get it out without crying again I was so emotional. He just could not believe what I was trying to say. He heard what I said, just could not believe it, until I showed him the account on the website and the money. He wanted to thank her himself so he called her and you could hear the emotion in his voice as he also conveyed his gratitude to her.

So that is how our travels and holiday adventures, as adults, approaching what some might call our Twilight Years, but we prefer to call ourselves Recycled Teenagers, began.

The world of travel is now open to everyone, no matter what their means, and access to holidays is available in magazines, on the net, television adverts and programs, and therefore no longer in just the high street. So being tech savvy (well, I am anyway); we researched what we needed to do. After all, on a bad day I cannot manage steps as I walk with crutches and Mike now had his UC to consider!

Being an almost middle-aged couple (Mike rising 60 and me in my mid 50s) much had changed since we had traveled on our mother's passports!

Jacky asked to be kept in touch about the holiday, so we wondered how we could keep that promise to our generous benefactor, and then came the idea of the website.

How we became First Time Tourists

We decided the easiest way to for Jacky to see what we were doing would be to set up a website with a blog on it. That was the easy bit, the difficult bit was choosing a name for it, aka a domain name that no one else had.

The first thoughts that came to mind was the fact this was our first time, as adults, to experience a true holiday, it was our first time on holiday together too, and then we realised that there was going to be many 'First Times' throughout the whole experience so we knew that those two words had to feature in the name.

Then we went to the dictionary and looked up all the words for people who take part in holidays - grockles, (Cornish) emmits (Devon), sun catchers, leisure seekers, sun chasers, holiday makers to name but a few. We then looked up the words *'tourists'* and *'travelers'*.

According to the dictionary definition:-

Tourist - a person who is travelling or visiting a place for pleasure.

Traveller - a person who is travelling or who often travels.

Then I found a list on a website (https://www.thecareerbreaksite.com) and dissected it.

The green is statements we agree with, the red is statements we feel does not describe us and blue is neutral:-

1. A **tourist** doesn't mind being called a tourist.

(We are what we are)
A **traveller** does, very much.

2. A **tourist** wants to see all the sights.

We want to see all the sites, but we hope to find things off the beaten track too.
A **traveller** wants to see some, but also to find something interesting that isn't in the guidebook.

3. A **tourist** tries foreign food but acts like they're putting a grenade in their mouth.

We both are happy to try any food; however, because of our foibles we watch what we eat as at our age we cannot afford to spend three days on a toilet!
A **traveller** eats the local food with abandon and spends the next 3 days on the toilet.

4. A **tourist** takes photos of all the famous stuff.

Once again, we will do both. For us it will be about making memories, as this might be the only chance of a holiday abroad.
A **traveller** takes pictures of ordinary people and things and is rewarded by the locals with gratitude or puzzlement.

5. A **tourist** will go to McDonalds in a foreign country, with no shame.

We do not eat at McDonalds' in any country!
A **traveller** will go there too, but not tell anyone.

6. **Tourists** tend to travel in large groups or with their families.

This is neutral, although being on our own this time, we would never say no to a coach tour as in some places this might be the best way to travel for us
Travellers tend to travel solo, or with one other person, thus NOT BLOCKING THE PAVEMENT THANK YOU.

7. A **tourist** will learn a few words of the local language.

We would never pretend to know more that what we do, but we would do our best to learn something.
A **traveller** will too, but act like they know more.

8. A **tourist** gets ripped off.

11

My husband is a market trader, he knows all the current prices for just about everything so would never get ripped off, and he loves a good haggle.

A **traveller** haggles and still gets ripped off.

9. **Tourists** (the British ones at least) get drunk.

We don't drink alcohol.

Travellers also get drunk but ensure their drinking money is going directly to the local community.

10. **Tourists** go on holiday.

We do both

Travellers go travelling

It was close! But there you have it, we are the:-

FirstTimeTourists.Com

WELCOME TO

First Time Tourists

The Journeys and Adventures of a pair of Recycled Teenagers.

A Japanese Tour Guide consulting from the guide book

Miyako Meisho Zue written by

Akizato in 1787

Another meaning of tourists was from a dictionary, which recounted how things have changed though since then.

The world of travel is now open to everyone, no matter what their means, and access to holidays is available in magazines, on the net, television adverts and programmes and in the high street. So now everyone has the chance to be a First Time Tourist!

However, this does not mean that everyone has had a holiday, whether it is in their own country or abroad. Many reasons can prevent this work, limited funds because of illness and unemployment, raising families, the lack of knowledge of availability and cost.

We do not see ourselves as holiday makers, although this phrase was first coined in

1830-40, as most holiday makers today head for seaside resorts to bask in the sun during the day and party at night. We are not saying that they still do not do some exploring like Tourists, however; we see ourselves more Tourists than holiday makers.

So who are we?

We are a middle-aged couple in our mid too late 50s early 60s that are travelling for the first time as adults. Yes, we both had holidays as children but so much has changed since then we thought we cannot be the only ones to be in this situation.

So here we are, sharing our knowledge as we gain it, our adventures as we have them and giving you a glimpse of what you can do, even if you think you are too old to travel, or perhaps life has crept up on you and the body does not function as well as it used to, or you have some time on your hands and are ready to do something adventurous!

We will learn everything from this first holiday abroad so that we can then pass our gleaned knowledge on to others of our age, or even older, who believe they are too old, too disabled or think it is just too late to have a holiday.

Just start thinking of the world as your oyster! Or as Shakespeare so eloquently put it in The Merry Wives of Windsor.

Pistol: "Why then the world's mine oyster, which I with sword will open."

And so we started our 2013 Malta holiday in 2012.

So much to do, so little we knew..

14

CHAPTER 2

Or

PPPPP (Prior Preparation Prevents Piss Poor Performance)

Christmas is over and now is the time to prepare for THE HOLIDAY!

Mike has given up the stall in the shopping mall. The decision to do so finally made easier when he had a letter saying that they were almost doubling the rent! So, he found a stall in an indoor market and has moved everything into there. He appears more relaxed and definitely happier, and, being closer, means I can pop down and see him so I benefit too.

I have bought the domain name, moved it to the server, and I have uploaded WordPress. Over the holidays I built a lovely little theme and we are ready to go, everything from now on is an extension to what I wrote in the online the blog for Jacky that is, the holes have been filled in as the blog was kept short and to the point.

December 28th 2012

Travel and Health Insurance

Travel and Health Insurance abroad is very important as you never know what can happen, so I went on-line today to do some research. Now, I can remember seeing something about an E111 form in the Post Office in the past, so I put this into a search engine to discover it has been replaced with the EHIC, (this is the European Health Insurance Card) this will get you help at a reduced rate whilst on holiday, however, do not forget to get your standard insurance as well for costs that may not be covered by this as well as other incidentals like having to cancel your holiday, your luggage, personal belongings such as cameras.

Many people are confused by the concept of Travel and Health Insurance. Whilst you may only take hand luggage and therefore are not worried as there is nothing in the hold, this does not mean you can forget the travel insurance as it can cover you for such incidentals as stolen wallets, cameras, breakages and in today's financial worries, cover of cost coming home should your flight company go bust whilst your abroad, as well as cancellation if you have to cancel for various reasons.

With the health insurance, this can cover extra costs for specialist equipment, should it be required when bringing you home.

Luckily both Travel and Health Insurance are done through the same company, except that in Europe you have the bonus of the EHIC

Whilst we all believe that our holiday will be the best, it is not worth taking the risk of leaving things to chance.

To get your EHIC, go to the NHS site (https://www.nhs.uk/using-the-nhs/healthcare-abroad/apply-for-a-free-uk-global-health-insurance-card-ghic/)

I have done just that! And, after filling out the appropriate online forms I can now sit back and wait for them to arrive, yes, them, do not forget to do one each for everyone travelling in your party, or they can do their own, so remind them to do so as soon as possible.

Oh yes and the EHIC cards are valid for 5 years!

January 1st 2013 - Tuesday

Are Passports needed to travel in the EU?

One of the first questions we asked ourselves was "are passports needed for travel in the EU?" And the answer is Yes. Unfortunately, you cannot travel anywhere today without an up-to-date passport, however, as well as for travelling they are great for use as ID if you do not drive! But why are passports needed for travel in the EU? Very simple. It is the nearest thing we have to an ID card. And it is getting more difficult to get one if you have not had one before.

Mike got his some years ago, the theory being that we were to get married and then have a honeymoon, however, because of circumstances, his parents were working in South Africa when he was born, it took us 3 years to get his passport and to prove he is British too!!

So sidetracking for a moment, this is how Mike got his passport.

Mike's parents are British and his father was on a 4 years works contract in South Africa in 1952. He had taken his wife and the two children they already had, but whilst there, they had Mike. The 4 year contract ended and Mike returned with the family on his mother's passport with the other two children, into the UK when only 3. Got it so far? British parents have a child, ergo the child is British.

During the next 40+ years, Mike attended school in the UK, was sent his National Insurance number automatically when he was 16, served in the forces, got married and divorced, and has worked and paid taxes without being questioned about his nationality, until we applied for marriage. Much had changed since his first one. He was told that the driver's license was not enough, and so we started the process of applying for a passport. Off we went, filled in the forms and, again rather than send them, we decided to use fast track. Good job we did, we took everything we had at the time, which was the birth certificate Mike had been issued, but did not show his parents on, so we also had his mothers passport with his information on, his mother's birth certificate, his parents' marriage certificate, his father's birth certificate and yes, even his father's passport from back then, as well as a letter from his father stating that Phil was his son.

We were told to go away and get a proper certificate. This took three years of telephone calls, letters, emails and searching, during which we discovered that the place where Mike had been registered had burned down, complete with all the records. During this time we had been trying to call South Africa house in London, for which we had 5 numbers, one which was always answered by some girl and every time we got through her first words were 'everything is on the website'. We tried to tell her we were not applying for a passport, we would then ask if we could speak to someone but before we could finish the question, she would put the phone down. We phoned the other 5 numbers, but there was never any answer.

Meanwhile, we had moved from Bristol and had been living in a van and travelling from market to market. We continued to call the five numbers over the next 6 months once or twice a week at random times, and now and again we would call the number we had got from the website, but to no avail. We actually went through a period of time when we heard the authorities were checking peoples ID's in the markets and if they were not happy, the people were being sent back to their place of birth. This would not have made sense for Mike as he would, for all intents and purposes, be sent to a foreign country with which he had no links to at all!

So out of desperation Mike called the Nationalisation office, and this is how the conversation went.

"Good afternoon, Nationalisation Office, how can we help?"

"I am making inquiries about nationalisation" said Mike

"And what is the name of the person who wishes to be nationalised?"

"Mike Croft," answered Mike

"And can we speak to Mr. Croft, please?"

"You are speaking to Mr. Croft" replied Mike

"No, you do not understand, we wish to speak to the person who wishes to be nationalised."

"Yes, that's me." He seemed a little put out at this point.

"I am sorry Sir, but your accent is a giveaway, it is obvious you are British, we need to talk to the person who wishes to take the nationalisation test."

It was at this point that Mike was so obviously frustrated as he said.

"Please listen VERY carefully, I was born in South Africa when my father was on a four-year contract there. I came back with my British father and my British mother when they returned to the UK, I went to school in the UK. I received my national insurance card at 16, served in the army, and have paid taxes. Not once

have I had to prove I am British, but now they say I must so that I can marry my fiancée. Now over the phone you are telling me I am British. Please, send me the confirmation of what you just said so I can get a passport."

"Ah, I understand now, you are South African; the cost will be £700 plus VAT to do the test Sir."

At this point Mike just hung up.

He felt quite despondent, so called the Home Office, who said it was nothing to do with them despite HM Passport Office being run as part of the Home Office.

So we kept on doing the markets and I kept on making the phone calls to the South African Embassy

Then one day, one of the 5 numbers was answered, I literally begged the woman not to hang up, and she didn't. She let us explain everything to her and she told us to send all the information we had to her and that it would take up to 9 months to get a reply but to hang on in there. We did and she must have worked miracles because we had a reply within 6 weeks, Mike's birth certificate stating that it registered his birth that year! That meant that as a 55-year-old man he had only been alive since the registration, boy did that feel weird!

We got the passport forms and his new birth certificate which, in his own words, he would not let out of his sight. We drove to Wales again and this time everything went through. Except he now had to go for an interview to prove he was who he said he was. It was recorded; I guess to make sure all the photo's and ID were corresponding.

And then finally, after just over three years, Mike got his passport, and we were able to book our wedding.

But that was 3 years ago and we still have not got around to changing our names on our passports to our new lovely married surname. Mike had his name and mine hyphenated and had not told me so it was a lovely surprise when he said "I Mike (and our two surnames conjoined) take thee… etc", on the day, hence the passport updates.

Mine passport had run out and to top it all was still in my maiden name, and as Mike changed his surname to incorporate mine, we have taken this opportunity to renew both passports in our proper names.

So, how to go about getting a passport! There are two main methods 1) go to the Post Office, collect a form and fill it in or 2) apply online (https://www.gov.uk/apply-renew-passport) where you fill in the form and they send it to you to finish it.

The instructions are fairly clear, most important though is making sure you can find someone to do the verification, luckily we have a friend who is a teacher, however, if you do not have a friend who meets the criteria, don't worry, a doctor or solicitor will do it, but they may charge a fee.

Do not leave getting your passport too late! If you feel time is ticking by, and then instead of the straightforward send off you can do fast track or premium one day (https://www.gov.uk/get-a-passport-urgently). Here you make sure you have everything you need, and then, once you have it altogether, call and make an appointment. They will make this appointment for you at your nearest passport office. You can find this out when you call them to make your appointment, but remember, this costs more, so make sure you budget for it.

January 2nd 2013 - Wednesday

.Are we returning to Bristol?

We thought that returning with Ryan air would be the same as leaving, so there we were, looking at our incredible present when suddenly we noticed it. We were definitely flying too Malta from Bristol but for some reason beyond us; they decided we would be brought back to the UK, landing in Bournemouth! I did some research into train times, only to find that from Bournemouth to Weston-Super-Mare it came to over £70!!! And that was each! I quickly got on the phone to be told that to get back to Bristol would be a further £10 per person. I said I would just get hubby to transfer some money into my account and then I would call back to pay for it, which I did about an hour later. Now for some reason it is £60. I could not believe is as I then asked how come it had gone from £10 per person to £30 per person in so short a time, to be told there were no seats left and that we were being upgraded. Well, as it worked out cheaper, and easier, than the trains, I paid for it. Being first class and all that!!

Then I asked when the tickets would arrive. It is all done online and I have to check in 2 weeks before we leave. So we are all sorted now and looking forward to our holiday even more!!

January 3rd 2013 - Thursday

Applying for a passport

Knowing that applying for a passport does not always run smoothly, we went down to the Post Office today to collect the passport forms. We have decided that as we have only 7 weeks to go, we will do ours by fast track to save time. As mentioned before, there are certain criteria that must be met when applying for your passport, the least being that you must be a citizen of the United Kingdom, so make sure you have a full birth certificate with both parents' names on. You can get them from here https://www.gov.uk/order-copy-birth-death-marriage-certificate

January 5th 2013

EHIC cards arrive!

My word that was quick!! Barely a week and that included New Year's Eve, New Year's Day and a weekend to boot!!

Our EHIC (European Health Insurance Cards) arrived this morning in the proverbial brown envelope, two debit size cards easy to keep in the old wallet or actually with your passport.

We are getting rather excited now, as we cannot believe this is happening!

January 9th 2013

Passports - making the appointment

OK, well over the weekend a friend of ours, a teacher no less as I mentioned before, did the honours of signing the back of our photos and the back page of our passport application form, that is now sitting in the 'going away' (GA) wallet, with the details of the holiday.

Called the fast track number, (which can be found here https://www.gov.uk/get-a-passport-urgently) this morning, and lo and behold we both have an appointment tomorrow at 2pm in Newport!!

Got a list of everything we need to take and put it all into the GA wallet to take with us, received a text message from the passport office confirming time, place and reference number, and got £103 for each passport £3 for each return of certificates.

This time next week we should have them on the door map!

January 10th 2013

Newport Passport Office

Well, the day dawned for us to deliver the forms to the passport office; it was very misty and murky, but that did not deter us as we set off at 11 am for Newport.

I thought I would have a little play with one of the camcorders, but there was barely anything to see!

As we went over the Severn Bridge into Wales, you could hardly see the top of the bridge!

We got to Newport, parked up and then had a bowl of soup at a small cafe as we had time to kill, and it was rather nice soup! I had the parsnip and Mike had the tomato and basil. After he had added his pinch of chives and Parmesan cheese, he said it tasted just like spaghetti Bolognese, without the meat! Sounded delicious!

We were 40 minutes early for our appointment, but the man on the metal detector was really jolly and let us both in no problems, we went to the desk where we received our ticket, popped into the lift to the 4th floor and had only been in there for 3 minutes when they called us! Okay, no problems today. Just one silly question the woman had to ask. Why did I change my name twice on the same day??

I had to explain that as a wedding gift for my fiancée, as he was back then, I had my first name changed to the nickname he had always called me by, ok she understood that, but despite the marriage certificate being in front of her she was still confused as to why I had then changed my surname! Mike explained that's what happens when you get married, you take on your husband's surname, of which as a surprise to me, he had his name and mine hyphenated just before we got married, so I did not lose my surname!

So picking up all the relevant certificates off she toddled to ask if this was ok, we think anyway, so we waited and about 10 minutes later she called us back and said that not only was everything ok, but we would receive our passports in the next 7 days!!We popped over to the cashier, paid our dues, and left for home… or so we thought!

Coming out of the multi-storey car park, we were just approaching the intersection when Mike pulled the car to one side and put on the hazard lights. The accelerator pedal was not working, luckily there was a small garage across the road and the guy came out and told us the accelerator cable had snapped! I could not believe our luck, like we really needed this now, yet thank heaven it had not happened on the motorway home! Mike called the insurance people, explaining I was on crutches and had difficulty walking, and then we waited for a pick up vehicle.

We sat in the car watching the rain as the heavens had decided enough with the mist, let's give them some good old Welsh rain now, oh and lets drop the temperature a few degrees too! Eventually a low loader arrived, the car was put onto the back and the poor guy driving could not believe it as he had been told there was only one passenger, and then to discover that there was two and one of us needed a, um, a hump into the front of the very, very high cabin! Good old Mike, putting shoulder to task after lifting one of my legs onto the first step, and boy did he heave! I shot up and almost straight into the cabin on my nose! I hope he didn't injure his back.

We arrived safely home, Mike's back was fine, the car is now parked up and tomorrow she will be sorted. And now we just wait and watch the post!

January 12th 2013

Passports Arrive!

Mike was looking out of the window and saw a small white van pull up. Being the nosy people we can be at times, I walked over to watch as the man got out and walked towards our door.

"Ah, probably the return of our marriage certificate and name change deeds" I said.

I was at the door just as the man knocked. I opened it and looked at the two envelopes in his hand.

"Your passports," said the young man "please sign here."

I signed and went back up the stairs; I must admit we were both flabbergasted at the speed at which they had been done. We thought more like next Wednesday or evening Thursday! But no, we now have them in our hands, all safe with the **EHIC** cards in the travel wallet.

Oh and all our certificates were in the envelopes too so win win!

January 14th 2013

We are insured!

We had decided to save as much as we could so that we had back up money in the bank as well as what Jacky had given us. We were keeping that for backup in case of incidentals that cash was needed for. I had done a lot of research on the Internet regarding insurance, especially with all our foibles between us. I had picked a company that not only had an excellent reputation but had been around for some time and was also well recognised, namely Insureandgo.com.

So with relevant information, names, DOB, a list of illnesses, and our camera information I logged on and the glorious thing is that I could download everything off the net as soon as I had paid for it! However, I also clicked a button for having the information posted to us as well, so it will be interesting to see how long that takes to arrive.

Be warned though, you may need to go through a few companies before you find the one that suits you and your pockets as we all have different health issues.

January 20th 2013

To drive or not to drive?

One of the big issues that people seem to have is how to get to the airport and home again after the holiday. Well, we did some research and believe it is down to several factors, the main one being, how far away from the airport one lives.

We thought about a friend or a member of the family, but then we decided that might not be easy, no matter how good a friend is, if their alarm fails to go off, or they are running late due to prior commitments, in fact any little thing that is not really their fault can happen, and then this puts a strain on things.

Next thought was a taxi. With that there was the cost, £25 to £35 there, then the same to return home. Seemed like too much money to us, as well as the fact they will want to go their way and we might want to go a different way, so we ruled that out.

Copyright geograph.org.uk

Then we looked at airport parking, and this proved the winner. We booked over 7 days in advance, so this meant it was only £29.99. There is a free bus from the car park to the terminal, and we can leave whatever time we want in the morning, go by whatever route and when we get back, drive at our own pace. It's a winner!

So we have booked our space and also the added extra of 'Fast Track security' (we think it will help, not too sure but will let you know when we do!), and have printed off our tickets from the email we were sent so that is taken care of now.

January 26th 2013

Luggage

We did the research to find out what we may take with us.

Apparently Ryan air does not like you to take much!! And any extra has to be paid for!

So, you are allowed to carry up to a 10kg bag/rucksack/flight bag but it must be 55cms by 40 cm by 20 cm, any bigger, even by a cm and they will put it into the hold with a £60 fine! Sorry, not fine, that's what it will cost you.

So we have treated ourselves to a new rucksack, as we really need it, for me to carry as it is easier being on crutches and I want to do my part too, I cannot leave everything up to Mike, and I got a smart pull along for him. Once ordered, they were on the way.

Should be here by Saturday, according to eBay!

January 29th 2013

Things are arriving now.

OK, this may not sound very exciting to some, but my white summer socks arrived today!!

The first of 7 little parcels we are expecting this week.

Why white and ankle? Well, it has been a long time since I have worn anything nice in the summer as we are usually working, so I
thought I would treat myself!!

Wonder what will come tomorrow?

January 30th 2013

And more arrivals!

We had been out for a drive and as we pulled in we saw the wheelie bin had been moved to stand in front of the front door. We got out of the car and, in moving the wheelie bin back to its position; we revealed a package, turned out to be Mike's flight bag. Then we opened the front door where there were 3 delivery cards on the floor, which means a trip to the post office tomorrow morning, as well as a tiny package. It felt like Christmas all over again!

Copyright FirstTimeTourists.com

24

It was a tiny package and on opening it we saw it contained HIS swimming trunks!! Does spandex roll up small or what! I have been with him now for nearly 11 years and this is the first pair of trunks he has ever had all the time we have been together; he has promised to give me a showing tonight!

February 1st 2013

Getting worried now...

We have been doing some research into our holiday and we discovered many things about Ryan Air, a lot of it is scary.

For example the size and weight of your luggage as mentioned in the previous post. These rules are so strict! A woman cannot carry a handbag, unless it is her ONLY hand luggage, otherwise it must go into the handheld luggage.

You have to book your hold luggage on and there is a further charge for that.

Booking cannot be done until you sign into their website with the username they have given you. And you could not sign in until 2 weeks before you go!

If you do not print off the boarding cards properly, they will charge you £60 to do it at the airport!!

If your hand luggage is just over or does not fit into their special checking in cage, then they will again charge you £60 for it to travel in the hold.

So we decided - we are going to write to them to ask them lots of questions including querying the one that says you cannot take liquids on board, but if you want a drink of water, it will cost you £2.50 for a normal .25p 500 ml bottle!!

We shall let you know what happens on that one!

Oh yes, one more thing, they do not allow duty-free bags on board either, that has to be included in your hand luggage quota and be put into your hand luggage bag!!

February 2nd 2013

Check list!

If there is one thing I have learned since starting this, it is to make a checklist... of just about everything!!

So here goes ours:-

- ✓ Passports.
- ✓ EHIC.
- ✓ Insurance.
- ✓ Airport parking.

- ✓ Flight tickets.

- ✓ Hotel booking information.

- ✓ Correct size flight bags, check size and weight allowance.

- ✓ Does someone know where you are going and staying? Make sure you leave that information with someone for emergencies.

- ✓ In this day of technology, take a cheap phone with only necessary numbers and a PAYG (Pay As You Go) sim card.

- ✓ Wallet to keep all paper work in that needs to be carried.

- ✓ Envelope, one in suitcases one in hand luggage, with copy of all necessary paperwork especially passports.

- ✓ Suitcase, check weight allowance.

- ✓ Address of Consulate, and copy in copy envelopes.

- ✓ Prescription tear off of all medications, copy in copy envelopes.

- ✓ Check that there is enough medication being taken not just for length of holiday, but an extra week as well. NB if you are a diabetic contact the airline and let them know you will be carrying sharps.

- ✓ Check to see if you need a plug adapter; if so add it to the list!

- ✓ Translator. This can be done in several ways with today's technology, App on a tablet or phone, a hand-held electric one or just a good old-fashioned book!

February 12th 2013

Big Scare!

So there I am checking my statement when I see the words XXRyanairXXXXX Stansted Arp!!

I panicked!! We cannot possibly be landing at Stansted! We are taking off from Bristol, so surely we will return to the same airport!

I thought they had messed up AGAIN!!

So there I am trying to call them at 7.45, at night, on the blooming 0900 number as I had done a little research and discovered there were only 2 seats left on the only flight out that day!!

In the end, I called the people with whom the holiday was originally booked.

PHEW!! It is where they are based!! I can breathe easy.. Until I noticed the name used for hubby was Mike, not Michael as per his passport, so tomorrow morning I have to call Ryan Air to change the name OR THEY WILL CHARGE YOU FOR THE PRIVILEGE! Let's hope there is no charge just for this!

February 13th 2013

20 Questions for Ryan Air

Well, not quite 20!

Some of the following questions may not seem necessary to everyone, but they are to us as we want to see what Ryan Air has to answer.

So I filled in the form and, yep, you guessed it, not enough room, only 500 characters allowed!!

So we are going to go to Bristol and see their representatives there and will update you when we get their replies.

Here is a copy of the original letter I tried to send them but will now take with us on Saturday.

Dear Ryan Air,

I wonder if you can help us out with a few queries. This is our first holiday since we were both children and many things have changed since then.

We are not totally; I believe the term is, computer literate, and our holiday was something we were looking forward to.

1) Will I be able to take my prescription eye drops with me in my hand luggage?

2) I have to wash my eyes with bicarbonate of soda twice a day (doctor's orders), what is the best way to carry it on board as; unfortunately it is a white powder!

3) I have already mentioned my crutches when I called and made contact a few weeks ago, where would you like me to store them once I am on board the plane?

4) How much is baggage for the hold and is that both ways or one amount out and one amount back?

5) Do you serve decaffe on the plane and if so, how much is it? If not, are we allowed to buy water in the duty-free zone to bring on with us?

6) Do you do meals on the plane and again, if so, how much?

7) Am I to understand that the one bag per person means we are not allowed to carry our duty frees in another duty free carrier bag? And is it part and parcel of our luggage allowance?

8) I had to call to change landing at Bournemouth to landing at Bristol, in fact why were we booked to land at Bournemouth in the first place? I do not understand. When I changed the flight to one landing at Bristol, I was told that the seats coming back from Malta were upgraded to First Class when I called as they were the only ones left (reservation number VM94QH), please can you confirm this.

9) Who keeps the booking pass? Do you keep it when we book in or do we hand it in as we board the plane?

10) Where can we put our bags once we are on board? Can they be put under the seat in front?

11) How do I make sure I get a seat next to a window?

12) We understand that we have to put our camera into the hand luggage; however, can we put the charging leads into the hold luggage?

I look forward to your reply and any other assistance you can give

Kindest regards

February 16th 2013

At Bristol Airport

We drove to Bristol this morning, and found 'silver car park' without looking for it as it was on the way to the main airport, tick one off the box!

We drove into the short stay car park, found a spot and walked along the front where we saw a sign for the silver car park pick up and drop off point, second tick!

We went in and looked for something that said Ryan Air; we saw it eventually along a row of counters and headed that way.

There was a woman there, and we asked if she could help us with a couple of questions. Her attitude came across as none smiling, sharp and abrupt.

We explained, laughingly, that we had not had a holiday since we were both 15 and our parents had taken care of all this sort of thing. Still no smile.

She answered several of the questions, pointed out where we could get our plastic bags for liquids from, and seemed very dismissive. She was a representative for several companies, including Ryan Air. Things were not looking good.

We walked over to area 21 where she had pointed for us to go to ask about the bicarbonate of soda. What a difference! The security lady sat there and laughed when we again explained how long ago we had travelled, how we had watched the programmes on the telly regarding customs and excise, and she totally understood our worries about the bicarbonate. She said to put it into a clear bag, if possible get some new still in the box with the label on and if they need to check it they will do it there and then and it will only take 5 minutes. We were chuffed to bits and left on a higher feeling than we had done with lady number one.

Then we went into where Ryan Air passengers go through to board. There was no one waiting to board or anything and we saw a Bristol Airport assistant talking to a Ryan Air lady, so I headed towards them, smiling. And they both smiled back. I started off by saying that we had not been on holiday since we were kids, in fact the last time I flew was when the 'plane' flapped wings, she laughed! Oh Boy! We knew then we were in luck.

She showed us where we could measure our bags, the BA man suggested we had assistance as this would guarantee us getting on the plane first as it could be a long walk with me being on crutches, this would mean getting to the plane on a minibus.

By the time we left them, we felt happy and confident in our first meeting with Ryan Air.

On the way out we read a sign about going upstairs and were chatting away when the security lady came bounding (er she was about late 50's early 60's!) over to apologise for not noticing I was on crutches. She pointed out to where the lifts were for us to use to go upstairs after we had booked in, where to go for the fast track, and also explained that we would have our shoes, hats (yes we were wearing THE hats today) and coats removed, but not to worry as it is only procedure.

We then all chatted for about another 5 minutes, and when we left, we felt really relaxed.

On getting home we had a discussion. I spent some time weighing all our stuff, and we have decided that we will not be taking hold baggage. Not worth paying the extra for in our minds, we can use the money for ourselves to have a good time.

And so we shall!

February 16th 2013

Back from Bristol Airport

This is the answers we received in Bristol this morning:-

1) *Will I be able to take my prescription eye drops with me in my hand luggage?*

Yes, but they must go into a see through bag that is regulation size with other gels, liquids and pastes, and none must be over 100ml

2) *I have to wash my eyes with bicarbonate of soda twice a day (doctor's orders), what is the best way to carry it on board as; unfortunately it is a white powder!*

No problem, just make sure it is accessible for the security check who may test it.

3) *I have already mentioned my crutches when I called and made contact a few weeks ago, where would you like me to store them once I am on board the plane?*

These will be put either in the overhead compartment or the nice steward might put them into their area for me

4)   *How much dose the baggage for the hold cost and for what weight? And is that both ways or one amount out and one amount back?*

15 kilos is £25 to go out and £25 to come back so that would be extra £50 OR 20 kilos is £30 going out and £30 coming back. Please note this is the low season.

5) *Do you serve decaffe on the plane and if so, how much is it? If not, are we allowed to buy water in the duty-free zone to bring on with us?*

Don't know, can't tell you, you can get water in the duty free but must be carried on board in hand luggage

6) *Do you do meals on the plane and again, if so, how much?*

No, but they do snacks on board again you can buy food in the duty-free zone but must be carried in the hand luggage

7) *Am I to understand that the one bag per person means we are not allowed to carry our duty frees in another duty free carrier bag? And is it part and parcel of our luggage allowance? And if I check in now, can I add luggage later?*

Duty frees must be carried in hand luggage, not an extra bag, it appears not to be part of the allowance, didn't answer the last one.

8) *I had to call to change landing at Bournemouth to landing at Bristol, in fact why were we booked to land at Bournemouth in the first place? I do not understand. When I changed the flight to one landing at Bristol, I was told that the seats coming back from Malta were upgraded to First Class when I called as they were the only ones left (reservation number VM94QH), please can you confirm this.*

Unable to answer this one as there is **NO FIRST CLASS** on Ryan Air

9) *Who keeps the boarding pass? Do you keep it when we book in or do we hand it in as we board the plane?*

We hand the boarding pass to the steward on entry to the plane

10) *Where can we put our bags once we are on board? Can they be put under the seat in front?*

Yes, they can be put either into the overhead compartment or under the seat in front.

11) *How do I make sure I get a seat next to a window?*

It was noticed I am on crutches and therefore was brought to our attention there may be a long walk to the plane so suggested I asked for assistance this will ensure we get on the plane first and can be settled next to the window before everyone else gets on.

12) *We understand that we have to put our camera into the hand luggage; however, can we put the charging leads into the hold luggage?*

No, you can put the leads etc into the hold luggage, the reason we ask for cameras etc to be in hand luggage is so that they do not get damaged in the hold.

February 24th 2013

Itinerary time

Being a Sunday and our holiday closing in on us, we decided that now was the time to sit down on our computers and work out an itinerary with costs, transport to the attractions, etc.

Our research revealed that Malta has many sights to offer from prehistoric to modern day film sets, and we really wanted to do it all but we knew that was not possible so we gave it a great deal of thought and decided that a cross section would be the best way to go. History places were many, and so we looked at the different cross sections. Medina called to us, its position being wonderful on top of one of the very few hills on Malta; the Tarxien Temples we decided would be our prehistoric visit with Valletta being the Middle Ages, and Popeye's village the modern day tour. There were a few other places to go to, but these three were top of the list.

February 26th, 2013

Money!

I did something I have never ever done before!! (Yes; I know there have been a lot of those over the past few weeks!!) We now have our money sorted!

We are only going to take about €200 and a savings bank card, nothing else as we feel that more than that is unnecessary. It felt fantastic walking down to the local post office, standing in the queue and asking for Euros! It brought home once again that we are going to another country.

When we get off the plane, we will get our weekly bus pass at the airport, and then the adventure can truly begin!

March 5th 2013

The Hotel

No, we have not arrived, but we made a big decision. On looking up about the hotel, we discovered that there was a good possibility that our room was going to overlook a lift shaft. Unfortunately, neither we nor Jacky knew this, so we let them know we wanted to upgrade ourselves.

I called the hotel and asked if we can be upgraded to another room. The only ones

31

they have are ones that overlook the harbour and it would be £125. I looked across at Mike and he smiled at me, "Go on, do it," was all I needed to hear to upgrade. I signed into my online banking and bingo; we now had a room at the front of the hotel overlooking the harbour. So expect lots of pictures of this from first thing in the morning to last thing at night!

Now this may or may not be an actual picture from the hotel, although the link said it was, however, we will replace it with an actual picture of our own as soon as we can.

March 6th 2013

All packed up

That's it, everything is all packed up and ready to go..We set the alarm for 5 am. The car has fuel in and the lights have been mended so nothing need stop us on our way.

A little present has been popped into the bag for Phil when he wasn't looking, I so hope they do not want us to empty the bags at the airport as all the cameras are packed in with bubble wrap nice and neatly and I really do not want him to see the present before we get there, defeats the object!

I have access to one of the camcorders so might try to film us taking off and landing and perhaps see if we go over Mount Etna too!

I wonder if we will sleep tonight.

I wonder if we have forgotten anything.

I wonder...oops Mike just called me to stop wondering and get to bed as it will be a long day tomorrow!

Well, goodnight one and all, the real adventure for us starts tomorrow!

CHAPTER 3

or

Leaving home and arriving in foreign lands

We were up before the alarm went off, which really surprised neither of us as the anticipation and adrenaline of new things to come had been coursing through us now for 3 months!

I put the kettle on and looked out of the window, it's raining, but we don't care!

We dressed in our 'going away' clothes, drank our coffee, got into the car and drove to Bristol Airport without incident leaving our every day stresses behind, however, at Congresbury we passed what appeared to be a 2 car side hit, but it did not appear serious and the emergency authorities were there dealing with it so we just carried on past.

With the rain still coming down we arrived at the Silver Zone Parking, found the disabled area and pulled into a bay almost right next to the reception doorstep.

The staff in reception was brilliant. We presented our parking receipt; they found our registration, put a label on our keys, gave us a receipt for them and even lent us a staple gun so we could staple the receipt to the print off booking form which we then put into our folder safe for when we got back home.

We offloaded our bags, did one more check for all paperwork, and then sat back and waited for the bus.

The airport bus arrived soon after, they run every 20 minutes, and we got on. There was plenty of seating for disabled, lots of space for luggage and plenty of standing room for everyone else.

As we sat there waiting for people to get on, Mike felt his face newly shaved face.

"I feel like a Specsavers advert," he commented.

"Why's that?" I queried.

'Well, after having to shave off my beard, it reminds me of the advert with the sheepdog.....and I feel like that poor sheepdog.'

Mike has always had some sort of beard since I met him; however, he had been so excited he had forgotten to book an appointment to have it trimmed, so he had a go at it himself. A little here, a little there, and next thing, he had taken the lot off. He kept his mustache though so did not feel too naked. The bus arrived at the airport. We got off, went in and headed for the checking in area of Ryan Air. We admit we were a little early; it was now only 06.10 am. Looking across to the check in, we saw there was no one there. Glancing around though, we saw a notice which said that if you have only hand luggage and no hold luggage to go straight to departures.

We went towards the lift, however, on glancing towards the stairs where we had stood the previous week we noticed the escalator was now working so headed towards that instead.

Getting to the top there were two entrances. One was marked fast track, so that was the way we went. We got through with no problems, producing our boarding passes and passports, and being shown the way to go to the scanners.

We removed our liquids and pastes, took off watches and bracelets, putting them together with our wallets and coats into a plastic box, we then removed Dinky my travel notebook (a small laptop), the Kindle (lighter than books) and Mike's tablet from the black rucksack and put these into their own box, this was then were sent through the conveyor belt scanner together with the bags and we went through the body scanner, which Mike set off. He had forgotten he still had on his belt buckle and was sent back to remove his shoes as well. Meanwhile, my sticks were stripped down and sent through the conveyor belt scanner as well.

Once we had our coats back on we walked through the duty-free area, noting the prices and thinking that we were not here for that as we continued to following our noses upstairs to where we could smell coffee in a Restaurant. One coffee later, we both felt a little more human! Luckily they served decaf!

The weather stayed horrible. Looking out of the windows from where we sat in the restaurant, we could see a low mist and rain. After our coffee we got up and looked around, walking closer to the windows and looking through them we saw a Ryan Air plane. We later discovered it was ours! We also watched one taking off, and it only took seconds before it disappeared into the mists they were so low.

We continued to wonder around the airport to get our bearings when we saw the sign saying 'assistance this way', so we followed the arrow and came to a desk where a lady asked where we were going. We told her Malta and our flight number, and she said to come back at 9.30.

We went off to find some water, which we found in Superdrug, then went back upstairs to while away the time reading and people watching.

There was a group of ladies all dressed pink in with pink wigs on. Apparently it was someone's birthday, and they were leaving the UK to foreign realms to celebrate.

Suddenly we saw heads turning and people parting. It was like the Virgin advert, as a group came towards us dressed in red and blues and other airline colours.
It wasn't until they got closer that we realised they were all men dressed up!!

We think they might have been going on a stag party somewhere and wondered if they were going to be on our flight.

Mike decided that as we had a good couple of hours to go that now would be a good time to have breakfast as we would not be eating on the plane or until we got to the hotel. He got up, found somewhere amongst all the cafes that did an affordable breakfast roll each and we sat there, eating our last English food for seven days watching the world go by.

The time came for us to wander down to the assistance desk, and on the way we brought some boiled sweets. I remembered as a child my mother telling me to suck a boiled sweet as we took off to stop our ears from popping.

We arrived at the assistance desk where we were asked to sit with others to wait for the person who was to help us and show us the way to the plane. After 10 minutes a lovely airport man asked everyone their names and then he led us off. There were 6 of us in total, 3 disabled and their carers who in our case and one other couple were the spouse and in the third couple it appeared to be an elderly gentleman and his son. Two of us were on crutches whilst the elderly gentleman was in a wheelchair. We followed the airport man through the doors, outside and then into gate 9b, meanwhile the rest of the people were heading for gate 13.

The wait was not long before we saw a square vehicle come and park outside. People got out the back onto a platform, which was then lowered to the ground. After they were all off, it was our turn to get onto the platform to be raised up so we could get inside and sit on the seats provided.

We were driven to the rear of our plane where the front of the bus connected to the plane and we walked on, straight to the seats which were reserved for the disabled.

(we did not get a photo of the actual life but this is similar to it)

It was sinking in. We were now on board the plane. I had let Mike sit next to the window. There was a reason for this, as will be explained in the next little story.

Now, Mike can be a bit of a joker at times and as the people were boarding the plane he suddenly sat upright and asked where his parachute was. Knowing him as well as I do, I played along.

In a very gentle voice I responded, "what do you need a parachute for dear?"

"Why to get off the plane, of course!" was his response.

"The plane will land in Malta and we will get off the way we got on." Was my sensible reply.

"Don't be silly. You know planes don't land. I need a parachute on to jump out the back."

I was finding it difficult to keep a straight face.

He was looking under his chair now and muttering to himself. Thankfully I knew he was being his usual funny self and of course, with all the excitement I think it just made him worse!

"Now dear, look out the window, you can watch us take off." I told him.

"Window? Since when did planes have windows? And I still cannot find the parachute," was his response.

I reminded him again that planes land.

"Now you are being ridiculous," he said "when I was in the army you had a parachute, jumped out the back and the planes just flew off into the night. They never land"

It was at this point that I could not contain myself; I giggled and putting my hand into my pocket where I had put some Smarties earlier, tipped some into my hand and said, "There you go, take your tablets. You will be fine" before creasing up with laughter. I think some people heard us, but if they did, they must have been laughing too because all I could hear was tittering coming from other seats.

And this was the reason I let Mike sit next to the window for takeoff, he had at that point in his life, never been on a plane that had landed or had had windows!

The plane was finally loaded, and the engines roared and as it slowly moved off I took out the video camera and panicked. The battery was now running low! I had been recording everything that moved!

We popped our sweets into our mouths and sucked them as the plane slowly turned, then stopped as the plane in front took off. Then it was our turn, the engines got louder and suddenly we were moving fast and faster, the front of the plane tipped up as we took off and we looked at each other as the force pushed us back into the seats.

I leaned back and told Mike to watch out the window. He had never seen the way a plane goes through the clouds and then out the other side, and suddenly bright sunshine hits you.

He watched out the window intently. Unfortunately, the cloud was very thick, and we were in the air for 20 minutes before we were above the cloud line. And did he smile!

His face lit up like a young boy, I thanked my lucky stars that I am married to a man who can express himself when he is experiencing something for the first time, rather than someone who feels that because they had seen it on the TV, they had decided it is nothing to get excited about. We made ourselves comfortable, with Mike taking photos of the cloud formations, and then he played solitaire while I read.

Unfortunately, I eventually had to spend a penny and off I went. It was not too bad, but I really must lose some weight, tuning around in these tiny cubby holes is certainly an experience. I am sure they were bigger when I was younger, as all things seem to be when you are a child!

When I got back to our seats, Mike made to move, but I would not spoil his day, (nor mine I love watching him smile) so I sat in the middle seat and he remained by the window.

I started typing on Dinky when he asked me to look down at the snow and asked if I could see the mountains and snow below, I explained that France would have snow inland and I did not think we were over the mountains yet.

Twenty minutes later I glanced out the window with him, and we both said, "The Alps!" and yes, there they were!

Ryan Air was selling some lottery tickets, so we brought a packet each, and he won 1 new scratch card and I won 2, we exchanged them and I won another one. So now we have 4 tickets to send off for a chance to win a million!! Yeah!!

One hour to go and we were over the Mediterranean, so much cloud, but we got the odd glimpse of something. I hoped it would be clearer when we come back so Mike could see more land! He turned to me at one point and told me he had seen a plane below us and it looked like a tiny toy that they put onto model railways, only smaller!

The clouds were breaking! The Mediterranean Sea looked wonderful, a little turbulence but, hey, the views were magnificent! I wonder if we will see Etna?

We looked out of the window at what we believed was Sicily. Hooray!! Mount Etna was behaving herself!

Then the Captain announced we were due to land in 30 minutes, could everyone please return to their seats, fasten their belts and make themselves comfortable. Mike helped me back into my seat belt, and then we spent the next 20 minutes watching out of the window. We banked left, then straight, and then on the second banking left we caught our first glimpse of Malta. The buildings seemed to be made of white and yellow stones. We both felt very emotional–or was that our ears popping as the flaps were lowered as we flew over blue and aquamarine waters.

The plane leveled up as it came in for the approach, with the engines roaring as it came into touchdown and then the bouncing and finally the smooth run up to the buildings.

Then came the scrabble for the hand luggage and the doors, but we just waited patiently as we saw the airport disabled transport lorry come over and connect to the rear door, and, removing our bags and my crutches from the overhead baggage area, made our way to it.

The Maltese assistances were lovely and smiling away as they helped us on board their disability lorry, the same kind we had used at Bristol. Then off we went and after a short drive we were at the airport buildings. The door opened, and we stepped out onto the hydraulic platform and with us on it were safely lowered down.

We all stepped off into the warm sun, so different from the rain and drizzle we had left behind in England, and followed the young man to customs where we had to show our passports. We then got our first disappointment. They may not stamp our passports. The customs man kindly explained that as we are all in the EU, by stamping a passport, this puts a time scale on how long you can remain in a country, and being part of the EU means there is no timescale. He was really nice to us when he saw our disappointment.

Then we went to the entrance where there was a young man with a sheet with our name on. We headed towards him and introduced ourselves. A woman, Ani, came over and told us she would meet us in our hotel at 1.15 in the afternoon the next day to confirm our lift back to the hotel and also to confirm about our assistance on the flight home. At this moment in time we did not question it, however, we were disappointed as we hoped to start our holiday in the morning with us only having 6 full days on the Mediterranean Island. So we then followed the

115 THE STRAND

Nice Things

driver to our mini bus with 4 others, got in and buckled up as we were now being driven through the streets of Malta.

Looking out the windows only confirmed what we had seen from the air. We knew we were somewhere different, exciting, and foreign, yet the young driver spoke excellent English as we weaved our way through the streets to arrive finally at our hotel.

We got out of the mini bus, retrieved our bags from the boot and walked through the entrance to be met by Pauline, the receptionist.

Speaking excellent English, she gave us some forms to fill in, namely the ones for upgrading our room. We filled them in and returned them, including the €140 for upgrade, and off we went to room 304. We travelled up in the lift which was all right for someone on crutches but I think would have been too narrow for a wheelchair.

The room was clean and smelled lovely and fresh. We were pleasantly surprised to find we were still self-catering. This really pleased us. Also we now had a small kitchen area, a dining room with a small table and 2 dining chairs, a sofa bed and a door through to our bedroom complete with balcony.

We went to put the lights on. There was no electric; however, on the side table next to the television there was a welcome book to the hotel. While I looked at that Mike rang reception, and just as they answered I found out how to turn the electric on. He informed reception everything was ok. We went to the apartment door and next to it was a slot. By placing the key holder into the slot, the electric came on. Voila!

Copyright 115 The Strand Sliema Malta

Then it dawned on us, this meant that we could only charge our batteries etc when we were actually in the room! (We have since discovered that Malta has one of the highest electric price rates in the world).

We unpacked, during which time I gave Mike the present I had brought for him, a sketch pad and some pencils. It was worth it as he went all sentimental on me. We then continued to make sure all our batteries were fully charged and then popped out for some milk, sugar and coffee.

On the way out we stopped at reception for two reasons, one being to find out where the nearest shop was the other to get our Wi-Fi (€25 for the week but there are also different amounts and times) and a key for the safe (we had found this in the wardrobe in the bedroom) €10 deposit, but peace of mind for the week for somewhere for our passports to be hidden. We were told the shop was not very far away so off we toddled, along The Strand, keeping the harbour to our left, 1ˢᵗ right, up the hill and there it was, on a small square.

We went in and straight to the deli counter for some Maltese cheese and bread. There was only one type of local cheese and they had run out of bread, so we got an ordinary sliced bread and some of the cheese, we also got butter (it was the cheapest option for a spread), grapes (enormous grapes), and of course the decaf coffee (100gms), sugar and milk. This all came to €14.10 (approx £12.2; I heard the purse groan).

We headed back to the hotel but this time, on the way back, we looked into the restaurants that lined the road. The food smelled tempting, however, doing quick conversions, we both agreed that it seemed somewhat expensive, but we chose one for our first evening on Malta to which we would come back later as it had been a long day and cooking was so not on the agenda.

As we entered the hotel to collect our key, (keys must be handed in whenever you exit the hotel) we saw a menu and, for a four course meal, the price was €9 per person, so out the window went the idea of eating out and we made our way to the desk where we made the relevant enquiries to be told that if we booked now, we also got a 10% discount too. So we booked and paid and were given a blue card to give to the staff on the top-floor restaurant where we would have our meal.

I then remembered our bus tickets I was going to get us from Arriva so I asked the receptionist where I could get them from and she pointed out the hotel shop to me. Easy! After paying €24 for our week's bus pass, and carrying the Wi-Fi username and password, the safe key, the blue card for our evening meal, our shopping and our hotel room key, we again headed for our room via the tiny lift.

Now, for some strange reason, the lift reminded me of the one in the film Thoroughly Modern Millie with Julie Andres where she has to dance or the lift would not work. I started to giggle and Mike wanted to know why and when I told him he agreed with me

When we returned to the room, I put the kettle on and Mike went into the front room, then I heard him call me. Until then we had not stopped to look out of the window that we had paid extra for, but Mike had been admiring the view while I was busy. It was awesome!

We have so much in common, Mike and I that immediately we started pointing things out to each other. To our left the harbour was full of boats of all sizes and types. From little fishing vessels to large pleasure boats, whereas straight ahead of us were big private yachts that were beached up on the other side waiting for the owners to declare 'summer is here' and to get them back into the water. There were also trip boats for rides around the Grand Harbour, something we made a mental note of.

The blue sky hung over Valletta at the mouth of the Grand Harbour again to our left, which is on the other side of Malta's capital. There was a cruise ship moored up on Valletta's harbourside, and across the mouth of this small harbour on our side is the long road along the front dividing Sliema from the water.

I made us a cup of much needed tea which we drank on the balcony; the weather being balmy and definitely drier than the UK! We took some photos and then as it was only 17.30pm (Malta time which meant we had now been up for 13 hours) we were feeling a little worn down. Mike got out Dinky (the mini PC we had brought with us) and tried to get online, so he popped off downstairs to get it sorted and I sat on my bed reading my Kindle and trying not to go to sleep.

Six thirty arrived, and we toddled off to the dining room on the 8th floor. Mike mentioned something about students, but then we changed the subject totally as we smelled the food. We left the lift, which opened up into the dining room where we were told it was all self service.

So we started with some lovely home-made carrot soup. We thought we would have some bread to go with it so we picked some up, however it tasted just like Madeira cake, and probably was. It really tasted very nice with the soup! Then we both had chicken, vegetables and potatoes and some sort of rice balls.

During the meal we came to the same conclusion. We would eat at the hotel every night as it was not only affordable, but delicious and, through watching others, it appeared you could eat as much as you like!

We asked a young lady if we could wrap up some of the Madeira type cake to take to our room to have with our coffee and she gave us some clean napkins to use. We returned to our room where we had the coffee but put the cake to one side.

It was now 9pm and as Phil was taking even photos, I was writing in the diary ready to transcribe when I get home.

Oh yes, and did I mention the students? Yes, there were about 14 of them. Some are in the room opposite us, and as I write this, they are getting to be a little noisy. Hey ho! I will let you know what happens tonight in tomorrow's write up.

So, good night one and all, and sweet dreams.

CHAPTER 4

Or

Our first day in a strange land

We had a fairly good night's sleep, although the beds were a little hard, but I guess we were just truly pooped after our long day before.

We woke up about 6.30am and I got out to see what the weather was like outside. Big Mistake!! The sun was incredible, and we discovered that our room faces east! The curtains were fantastic as I dropped them back in place and we soon re-accustomed to the light of the room.

After the yellow walls and sunspots had calmed down, I went and got our breakfast ready in the mini kitchen, 2 slices of toast each, Irish butter, Maltese cheese, mushroom, olive and pepper mix in oil, 2 bits of Madeira cake we had from the restaurant last night, grapes and coffee. I have never seen Mike put away so much for breakfast before! His normal breakfast being one, possibly two, slices of toast with peanut butter and a coffee. We then sorted out the cameras and batteries etc before leaving the hotel for a little meander at eight thirty.

We knew we had to be back for one fifteen to see the rep. We already felt as though the first day had been ruined, as it meant we dare not get on a bus to explore, so we decided to just go within our immediate area. Walking can sometimes be a pain for me despite the crutches; anyway, surely nothing could happen that would stop us getting back in time for the all important meeting!

We left the hotel and crossed the road, heading for the promenade, when we got jumped on by Greg and Caroline. Now let me explain what I mean by jumped! All along the seafront are brightly coloured booths where people stand from 9 in the morning till 3 trying to sell tickets for tours of the Islands that are Malta, Gozo and Comino either by coach or boat, to holiday makers. And two of these people are Greg and Caroline.

Greg started in with the sales pitch, and we must admit he was very good at it when we could. We explained we already had our Arriva tickets and that we were waiting to meet up with the rep. He said to watch out for the rep as all they would do is sell us the same tours but at astronomical prices. Again we thought this was just a ploy, but we went along with it. We then got chatting about where they were from, which was the UK as many ticket touts are, apparently! They were a nice couple and very friendly, however; we explained we were not looking for tour tickets right now as we wanted to see what this woman had to say, but, as Greg had promised discounted tickets on the ones they sold, we promised we would be back. We parted company on good terms, all laughing and smiling, and so we meandered on, keeping the harbour to our right this time.

When we left them, we walked up along the front, and, as Greg had said, nearly all the ticket touts where English with some Scottish ones thrown in as well. Finally, we crossed the road and, coming to a little piazza, we decided to be brave and ventured into the interior.

The street was fairly narrow and all the houses and shops were built of the same yellow sandstone bricks, not small ones mind, quite large, and all about 3 to 5 storeys high, cutting out the sun, but it was still warm to us.

Up we went and then we turned left, following our noses until we found a very small food vender sunk into the wall. The seller was an Eastender (from the east end of London, of course) who sold a Maltese delicacy of Spinach and Anchovy pasty. We popped one into our bag to eat for lunch later.

We continued with our walk up the street and then turned right, and looking down the street we saw the sea again and realised we were now on the other sea front at the top end of Sliema. As we walked along, we saw some old buildings now in ruins.

Once on the promenade we took a time check and decided that we still had plenty of time for a longer walk, and as we were not pushing it, I was feeling happy to go along with that.

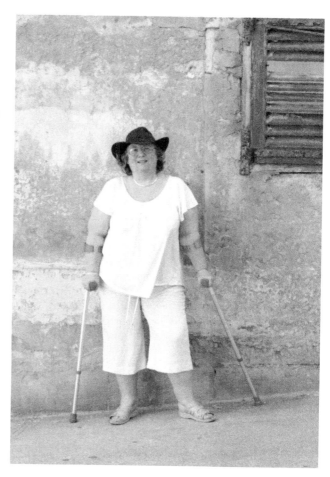

The sea was a lovely blue colour; the sky was clear, and we were nice and warm, not too hot, but just right, as we wandered along, looking into the small cafes on the seafront and surprised that although there were plenty of hotels along this area, there were no ticket touts.

And so admiring the view, breathing in the lovely salt air. Before we know it, we had been 'kidnapped'. Well, that's what it is called by those in the know!

Kidnapped

Louis approached us. He seemed yet another nice English guy, so we said 'hello'. He asked us who we had flown out with and we told him Ryan Air, to which he responded, very excitedly, 'that's the people who I work for!' then proceeded to ask how the flight went and where were we staying. At this point we saw no reason not to say, so we told him and he then offered us two lucky draw tickets, no catch.

Mike noticed the sleight of hand as Louis took a ticket from the top, which he handed to me, and one from the bottom, which he handed to Mike. Louis then got me to open mine first which said I had won a bottle of wine. We explained we do not drink alcohols per se, and he immediately handed me a small box inside of which was a lovely little gold coloured Maltese cross on a chain. We noticed he took this out of a leather 'tout' bag.

He then asked Mike to open his. Mike said he had won £300 worth of holiday vouchers, a free voucher for bus tours, and it was then that Louis got all excited and said it had never happened to him; someone winning this prize from his tickets. He said that to claim them we would need to go into the hotel across the road so he could sign for them; it was then that the idea that there was more to this than meets the eye, so we looked at each other, and Mike nodded at me.

Mike then asked if this was a Timeshare scam, to which Louis replied Timeshare is illegal on Malta except for the Gold Bay complex which had somehow overcome this by saying the rock bed where they were building was on Gozo, and getting a Gozo postcode. He, that is Louis, would not try to sell us Timeshare, however, if we would just pop across the road and give about an hour of our time all this would be explained to us. Having nothing better to do, and also with Mike having been a national sales manager at one time and very curious about how others worked, I needed a rest, and there was a free cup of tea as well!! We went for it.

We followed Louis across the road and into the PreLuna hotel. On the way Louis explained we were going to be shown around the new hotel which had been built adjacent to this one, but which we had to access through the PreLuna. He was quite insistent that the PreLuna had nothing to do with the new hotel next door at all. We looked at each other as Louis went off to arrange for us to sign for our vouchers and also our free cup of tea.

We looked around and could not see any signs of building work. It was definitely a pleasant hotel, and we also discussed the fact that what appeared to be the 'building

46

next door' was accessible through a rather nice, permanent looking archway. We discussed the idea of this being some sort of scam and, as we are both naturally inquisitive people, were looking forward to when Louis would return, which he soon did.

Now, just a word here. Normally we would not waste a scammer's time, but this was for research for the blog and for our experiences to share with you.

Leading us through the archway he now declared we were in the 'new hotel' and that it was only accessible by lift, so in we got.

At the third floor we all got out and, just to the right of us, in a corner were a desk and some chairs, Louis asked us to sit on the chairs while he went to get Pauline. Pauline arrived and the first thing she did was to sign Louis's book. He was really excited now, going on about the fact he had not only got €30 but a paid day off as well! He then handed us the vouchers which he had taken a note of the numbers of, as had Pauline, and then he was off.

Pauline then proceeded to ask us to show her the tour ticket and the cross, which she then pulled over to her side and covered with some papers saying we would get them back after the interview. She then described what would happen next, that is, we would be taken into the room next door for a cup of tea and a chat with Paul regarding the hotel and its unique offer and reiterated again that this is not Timeshare as this is illegal on Malta.

Then she got up, picked up all the papers including our freebies and went off. We were then joined by Paul, a middle too late 50s man who was from Scotland and had come to live on Malta, I mean, as he said, who wouldn't want to it's a wonderful place.

He started off telling us about the 'new' wonderful hotel we were sitting in and how it was not quite finished yet and how he had such an amazing offer. Then he asked Mike what he did for a living, to which the reply was a trader and event organiser. Paul's immediate response was that 'people who do that always have lots of residual money'. (Would love to meet the person who told him that as we were waiting for this 'residual' money!)

Mike listened as Paul went on about the hotel and then stopped him.

Paul asked him why he was stopped and Mike explained that he had been one of the top national salesmen in a very large retail company with many outlets, and that what he was hearing was a sales pitch.

Paul asked us if we thought he was going to ask for money and if so how much, Mike said probably more than the €300 we had just won to which Paul said yes.

Paul asked us why we were there and Mike explained we had been somewhat railroaded and that as this was NOT Timeshare we became intrigued, however, as he had followed Paul's speech he became convinced it probably was.

Paul said it definitely was NOT Timeshare, as this is illegal on Malta. This seemed to be the mantra of the day around here. So Mike asked him bluntly what was it and how much.

Timeshare on Malta is now called 'holiday club' and it will cost you £15000 and as he said this so Mike said that we had wasted enough of his time and we were leaving as we were not interested in either, so Paul gathered up his papers, asked if we knew where the lift was and left the room.

We had been with them for nearly an hour now and still no cup of tea.

We got into a lift where there was a couple already there, from the 7th floor, we asked how the building was going on and they looked at us as though we were really weird and explained they had been coming to the hotel since it was refurbished in the 80's and that it was finished back then!

We left the hotel the way we came in and had a really good look around. There was definitely no building going on, neither outside nor in! (We have since discovered that it was finished back in 1969!)

We decided we must have had 'mug' on our foreheads as we walked further along the seafront, then realised we both stuck out like sore thumbs.

Everyone was wrapped up like it was the middle of winter, whereas we, and other tourists and holidaymakers, were dressed for summer! DOH! In the word of Homer Simpson.

Dr. Fish

After leaving the hotel Preluna, we both felt as though we had a bitter taste in our mouths. We mulled it over and then the sea on the beautiful yellow rocks caught our attention, so we promenaded. The waves were washing over the rocks as we looked out. This was the North side, straight on, and the next stop is Italy or Sicily if you miss by a few miles.

Malta is in Europe but funnily enough it is the most northern part of Africa's tectonic plate system so it only by pure chance it belongs to Europe and in those waters lurks one of the seas biggest killers, namely the great white, but we did not worry about that as they were not as dangerous as the ones in other places, and we were not going into the sea either.

The sun was shining; the wind was balmy and we could smell the anchovy and spinach pasty as it wafted from the backpack so, at ten o'clock, we sat on the seafront and, retrieving the now squashed pasty, we ate it. It was delicious. It filled the hole nicely, thank you.

We strolled back the way we had come, and Mike decided he was going to confront Louis.

Only once again we got distracted!

Bubbles!! What a lovely name we thought, then had a peek in to discover it was one of those places where they have fish to 'nibble' your feet!

We checked the time and saw it was only 10.10 so, in for a penny, in for a euro, and in we went.

Caroline met us straight away, and she was a very bubbly person herself. We were the only two in there, so she talked us through it. We removed our socks and shoes, sat on a stool and she washed our feet to remove dirt that may be there, also to make

sure we did not have any fake tan on or any sort of chemicals, then she placed blue plastic foot covers on our now clean feet, you know, like the ones they wear on a crime scene, and we walked over to where we had to sit for the 'doctor' fish to do their stuff.

Caroline removed Mike's covers first, and he gently lowered his feet into the water. Soon the fish were swarming over them

She then helped me to turn 90 degrees, took my covers off and I slowly lowered my feet into the water and the fish were soon around them too. The only thing is I am really, *really* ticklish, and trying to keep my feet in the water was almost, but not quite, impossible.

As we both relaxed, the initial ticklish feeling started to wear off.

Caroline brought us both a cup of tea, decaf!! And we all sat around chatting as once again, Caroline told us she was another ex-pat!

A famil y came in, 2 youn g girls and their parents. The youngest girl really wanted to try it so she, her older sister and her mum all had their feet washed, covers put on and were helped to sit on the seats over the aquariums. The mother was fine, the oldest daughter was fine, but the youngest was very nervous. Caroline understood and told us, quietly, that is always the way. She was very patient. The girl removed her feet and then sat talking to her father.

The family were from France and so, with their good English, and our limited but

49

understandable French, we all sat and talked about life in general.

Soon the young girl wanted to try again, and so Caroline helped her to put her feet back into the water. As the family's timers went off, she left the young girl there while she helped her older sister and her mother to dry their feet and get off the chairs.

They only had a 15 minutes session, and we had 30 minutes and soon our timer went off as well. We had been watching the fish all this time. There were about 50 in each tank and sometimes they would be half round one foot then half round the other, and then they would all suddenly go to one foot and concentrate on that one then all suddenly shift to the other foot. It was really funny to watch.

Mike dried his feet, put on his socks and sandals then came round to dry my feet and help me back on with my sandals We said goodbye to the family, goodbye to Caroline and, feeling like we were walking on air, we headed back toward the Preluna.

The Tour Operator

We meandered back to the hotel, but about ten yards down the road there was Louis, so Mike decided he was not happy about me having lost the Maltese cross and him losing the bus tour after being told we had won them fair and square, so he went up to Louis and asked if he would pop in and get them. Louis went into the hotel and returned about 10–12 minutes later, saying that if we were to lie… yes LIE about what we earned and then sat and listened to a one-hour lecture, oh yes as remember this is not Timeshare, then sign something we will get them back. It was at this point we decided we were right; it is Timeshare but hidden under a new name, Holiday Club. And so we left and headed back to our hotel.

We came out onto part of the harbour walk again and just pottered along as we still had some time to go until the meeting with the tour operator.

Then I saw some strawberries. Now being a Devon girl, I have a terrible sweet tooth for these luscious fruit, and these were luscious. Locally grown and picked, not

forced and right in the middle of the Maltese strawberry season. How could we resist! We didn't. We brought a punnet, no; we brought a large punnet and now all we needed was some real bread from a real baker. I asked the fruit man where we could find such a

place. He told us to go up the road on his left, our right, take the second left and follow our noses. And yes, he was right, that's all we had to do! Literally, just follow our noses!

Now up to this point we had asked several people, namely English, where we could buy some real Maltese food, and they all kept pointing to the local restaurants. We had all but given up anyone understanding what we meant, and when we turned left, we knew the fruit man had really understood what we had said, probably because he was Maltese.

And what a bakers! Open fire oven, hot and smelling of fresh bread. We brought ourselves a Maltese loaf and also 2 hot cross buns and started talking to one local. She was a lovely lady, and we walked back along the small street together, talking about the up-and-coming elections. This is the first we had heard of them, but it would not be the last I can assure you. With our faith restored, we carried on back to the hotel for our meeting.

We got there at the same time as Ani, who then told us about the tours we could do with her. We sat at a table and she went through the book with us, pointing out that the bus routes were circuitous; there was the north circle and the south circle. Then she explained the Arriva tickets we had were not worth it. We would take hours to get anywhere as these were local buses and we would have to travel with the local people so on and so forth. In fact, painting a not very nice sounding picture of the bus services on Malta.

She asked if we knew where we wanted to go and we both said that one of the places was, of course, Gozo. 'Ah' says Ani, 'no problem, you can do this for €55 each. This includes the bus there, the journey across on the ferry, and then half an hour in one place, and half an hour in another and then there is lunch and then back on the bus to continue the tour.'

We listened with interest as she told us about other tours, ones that Gregg had told us about at more affordable prices. During this time we tried our best to explain that we were not interested, but it fell on deaf ears as she went from one tour to another, trying to get us to buy tickets for at least one tour. We tried to explain that I cannot walk far and that I would hold everyone up, but she had an excuse for everything including that I could sit on the bus and wait for everyone, so I got cheeky and asked "Would that be half price for me then as I will not be seeing the sites?" Although said in jest, the response was the look on her face. She was expecting me to pay full price to just sit on a bus and see nothing of the places of interest. Mike and I looked at each other and nodded. Between us we mentally decided that was the last straw that in the decision that we would book no tours with Ani at such a cost.

In the end she ran out of steam and we said we would think about it. I think she understood as she gave us her card to make sure we called her when we knew what we wanted to do, so we could book. Then she turned to leave.

"Er, excuse me, but did you not say this meeting was important as it was related to our return flight?" asked Mike.

"You have booked that haven't you, as I see you have also booked a pick up for 4 am on the day you go home, so unless there is something you want to ask me there is nothing else?"

"So this meeting was not about our flight home?" I asked.

It was at this point that she said she was in a hurry and had to go as she was running late. And so she left.

We felt like once again we had been railroaded, only this time it was down to the booking agents who should have told us there would be someone there to talk to us about various tours etc giving us the chance to cancel so as not to waste the rep's time and our very little precious time. But we were learning.

End of a long day

After the tour rep left, we went back upstairs to our hotel room for a lovely lunch of Maltese bread, ham, a little leftover cheese and mushrooms, fresh strawberries and grapes. Again Mike eating so much!

After lunch I felt tired so I went for a lie down, seeing me asleep, Mike covered me with a blanket and went outside to chat to Greg and Caroline. Suddenly my sleep was interrupted by shouting and car horns. I went over to the balcony and saw 2 pink open top (tour) buses going up the main street full of, what can only be described as, screaming youths.

Looking across to the stands I saw Mike, and he looked up, seeing me he waved and came back to the hotel to join me. He asked if the noise had woke me as he had also closed the windows so I could sleep; I explained it had and then he told me what he had heard from Greg and Caroline.

> *"We have come at a really exciting time for the Maltese, according to Greg and Caroline. It is Election Day tomorrow (Sunday) and the Labour party has hired all the tourists' buses for Monday. The results are due on Sunday and what is happening is that Sliema's mayor is a conservative area and so the buses are full of Labour supporters. However, there is a possibility that on Monday the tour buses will be being used by the Labour party to ferry around their supporters, putting a tour out of the question, in fact we will probably be safer staying in on Monday as things may or may not be good, again depending on who wins, there will be lots of noise and possibly fighting"*

After telling me this, he then told me about the deal he had struck with Greg regarding a tour of The Grand Harbour, so we went online to transfer some money across to our holiday account. Only we could not get online.

We went downstairs hoping to get a better signal and whilst I was transferring the money Mike had been looking around and came back with some information regarding car hire.

We looked at each other as we did the maths. The tour buses were going to come to

€120 for four days (remember there are none on Monday!) if we wanted to do something every day, then there was the entry fees and the time limit as the first tour bus left at ten in the morning and the last at three in the afternoon, which would limit our day. Then we looked again at the bus routes. There was something missing, in fact several something's missing. There was no stop for Mdina, Dingli, Popeye Village, the Red Tower or Roscali Fort and the Med Studios! All places we had planned to see!

We looked again at the car hire; it was going to work out at €115 for five days, plus some fuel, and no doubt a returnable deposit. Things looked up. After all, on Malta they drive on the same side of the road as in the UK! What could possibly go wrong?

Mike went to the desk, and they kindly phoned the company for us. He explained the car would not be needed on Monday as we had no intentions of leaving the hotel and, well, what can I say! They said that provided he parked the car up in a safe place in the back streets and they are fully aware of the situation, and that we were doing the right thing, we could pay for 4 days instead! So now the hire would only be €92! Result! And they would send a vehicle to pick us up at 09.30 in the morning from the hotel.

Feeling a lot happier we walked up the road to where there was an HSBC Bank and tried to withdraw the money, nothing, so I made sure I was using the correct card with the correct PIN number, yes, I was. We tried again. It would let me get into the account but not withdraw the money. Now we were really worried, so we went back to the hotel.

I was close to tears at this point, wondering what else could go wrong, so we brought a phone ticket from the receptionist, went to the phones at the back and called the number on the back of the card.

It was at this point I got confused and the man on the phone said he refused to answer any of my questions as it was obviously NOT my account as I could NOT answer the security questions!

I was now in tears and Mike gave me a lovely hug. I took a deep breath and realised I had been answering the questions using the wrong account information, so I took another deep breath and called again. This time I got someone different, and I sailed through the questions. I asked why I could not take any money out, so he asked how much I was taking, I said €250. 'ahh' came the reply 'that's the problem! You're only allowed to take £200 per day!'

I hung up; breathing a sigh of relief, I turned and explained to Mike what I had done. Another DOH! moment!

As it was now 6.45 we went straight up for the evening meal.

Choosing soup again, we made sure we had it with bread this time, and again it was homemade and delicious! We followed this with a small amount of beef stew, brussel sprouts, and potatoes. When we had finished, Mike went back for some more! And a spoonful of pasta! I had some salad with a slice of cold omelet, an Italian potato dish, cheese, tomatoes and homemade potato salad.

Then Mike really surprised me. The dessert was a chocolate mousse, and, before I knew it, he had gone back for seconds and then sat there, grinning, like a naughty schoolboy! Anyone who knows Mike will understand why I sat there in shock, not only at him eating so much but grinning like that.

The dining room staff are really pleasant and were laughing when they asked if I wanted another one, but then laughed even more when Mike said no but they saw me helping myself to his though, all done in fun of course! After dinner we went back to the bank and got out the money. On the way back, we popped into the hotel shop for a look. I left Mike browsing while I went to get the room key.

He then joined me at the lift, showing me something he had brought. It was a small bottle of carob and orange liquor and a small bottle of an aniseed liquor to have in our coffee that night. I may have mentioned we do not drink alcohol as a rule, and this would be about the 3rd time in 10 years we would do.

Our coffee was delicious and to cap it all, I did not have an allergic reaction, which meant that there were no 'extras' in the liquor! Contented, well fed and comfortable, Mike sat on the balcony taking photos of the passing traffic, whilst I sat and wrote about today's adventures. And then we both went outside to take even more photos.

Finally, at about 11 o'clock we both climbed into bed and were soon asleep, looking forward to the car hire people picking us up in the morning.

So good night one and all and sweet dreams.

CHAPTER 5

Or

Who's for spinach?

The sun once again was glorious! Before leaving the UK we had done researched into the weather and it said it was going to rain or be very cloudy every day. So far the rain or clouds had not put in an appearance, and yet another day seemed to be avoiding the meteorologist's plans.

When we opened the curtains, we very carefully peeled them back to confirm the sun was there and then left them slightly ajar as we got up, dressed and then dined on Maltese hot X buns, grapes and strawberries.

Then, somewhat excitedly, we packed our day bag with cameras, covered ourselves in factor 50 to and went downstairs to wait for the car rental people to pick us up.

When we got down there, 15 minutes early of course, there was a, well normally I would say gentleman, but this guy was not being gentle in any way at all. He was swearing and having a go at Pauline.

It appeared that the, er, person in question was with a group of artists who had booked to come over from either Germany or Holland or somewhere like that going by his accent, and that he was not happy with the rooms as they looked over the courtyard and lift shafts. And artists MUST have a view!

We sat there and listened as he raved on and on, what made it worse is that he was well over 6ft tall, in fact Mike who is 6' 2" would have had to look up to him, and he seemed to take great pleasure in telling Pauline, about 5' 3" and petite, that the rooms "where sh** and there was no view" and this was not what he had been expecting.

Mike and I looked at each other and later confirmed we had both been thinking the same thing. When he paid €3.50 per night per person with the company he booked with, did he not question why the rooms were so cheap? Obviously not! He made some comments about how this would not have happened to him back in his country, artists would have been given rooms with views, and yes, they may have done, but not for that price!

Pauline, bless her, kept her cool and offered to upgrade anyone who came down with their bags in the next half an hour. Only 2 turned up.

The guy stormed off, and we asked Pauline if she was ok. She said that she is used to it. It suddenly dawned on us and one of us asked the question. "We take it that these people are happy to pay the price of the cheap room, but when they get here and find no view etc as they have done no research, they take it out on you and your staff not the tour operator?"

"That's right," came the reply.

We felt sorry for the staff then and realised how lucky we were we had looked up the information about where we were staying and then upgraded before leaving England. Don't get me wrong. The hotel is lovely and there is nothing wrong with any of the rooms, however, if you pay €3.50 for a room then there is a good chance there is no view! So don't complain!

It was at that moment an elderly gentleman came in and asked for us, so off we went to get our vehicle.

He drove through Sliema and off towards Paceville, Mike asking him questions about driving in Malta. Seemed pretty straight forward to me! Then the driver pulled off the road onto a small street and parked up. He pointed to the shop across the road where we went to finish signing for the vehicle, then we were asked about insurance, fully comp being €60. Again we decided this was best and was now well within our growing allowance.

All signed up, we went to get into our little car. Poor Mike poured his long legs in and immediately moved the seat back. Then he was comfortable.

I got out the map, and we decided that as we were heading to the top end of Malta, we would keep the sea to our right and nothing could go wrong.

It really was a lovely drive. We followed the road out of the towns and into the country. The walls were all dry stone and reminded me of Devon. The sea was an amazing colour, and the houses were all flat roofed.

Then we hit our first roundabout.

Now let me explain the difference between the UK roundabout and the Maltese roundabout.

First you know it is there, is saying so on the map. Then you are on it. Unlike the UK there are no warning signs, there are no signs showing how many turnoffs there are. There are no signs to say where the turnoffs go. In the UK you get warnings, you know how many turnoffs because it says so on the signs, and you know where the turnoffs go, it says so on the signs.

There are no white markings on the road in Malta; these have all been worn away over the years.

So the breaks were applied, as in the UK, to give way to traffic from the right, and that's when the first horns sounded. Apparently you do NOT stop, you carry on and put your foot down, then as you go round the roundabout, if you're lucky the first time, you will see the sign actually on the turn off for where you want to go, apply pressure to the accelerator and take that turning, not hitting any of the other moving traffic on the road if you can help it.

That was our first altercation. Adrenaline running high, Mike 'asked' me why I had not been watching for the signs. 'What bloody signs?' I responded.

We calmed down and carried on. Next roundabout. Same as before.

We were not sure now if there was a pattern to this, so we just went with the flow. Yes, we took a couple of wrong turnings, safer that way; however, the sea was always there on the right.

We went through a couple more towns and everywhere seemed quiet, except for large groups of people standing around. We then remembered it was polling day, and these groups appeared to be waiting to vote at the polling stations.

We also now know that the roads were quiet too.

One of the lovely sites we saw was a man in the water with his horse. It seemed like they were swimming together. We also passed two or three trotting carts on the road as well. A little like Ireland, we thought.

We drove out of St Julien, past Pembroke and along the coast to Il-Mellieha where again we turned off the main road and ended up going through a lovely town.

We had at that point realised we could not go too wrong, so carried on through and met the main road out the other side.

Then we saw the first sign that meant anything to us. 'Popeye's Village'. So turning off, we followed the road.

Literally.

We saw no more signs, so kept following the little red car in front, even when it went passed signs that pointed to the right, implying we had to drive on the wrong side of the road, but the car went left.........and so did we.

The road we were now on was lovely. No potholes, something the rest of the roads seemed prolific in, and so we carried on. The red car turned off left onto a track. And it was at this point we realised something. No one else was on the road. It was as wide as a dual carriageway. There were no lines. It was new. How funny if we turned the next bend to find ....OMG they ARE!! They were still building the bloody road! No wonder no one else was on it!

Mike did one of the quickest U-turns I have ever witnessed as I did a quick 'click' with the camera, for posterity of course!

And then we drove back down the hill and approached the area where we were meant to have turned off, only to see a sign saying 'Popeye's Village' facing us, but none facing the way we had originally come!

We turned off down the road, happily bouncing on the car's amazing springs to see clear blue water ahead and a small parking area with a cabin announcing we had arrived! And still in one piece, to boot!

At the hotel I had noticed some two for one entry tickets so, armed with one of there, I went in and brought our entry which was now €10 for two, although they had a special that day which was 10% off all entry, but I got the better deal.

We carried on through the cabin, down the steps, and turned right.

The sun was shining, there was a lovely warm breeze coming straight off North Africa, which I am sure we could see in the distance, or perhaps that was Lampedusa? Anyway, we rounded the corner and suddenly saw all the familiar houses as we took our first look at Popeye's Village, aka Sweethaven.

Popeye's village is fantastic!

There is a lot to see and do, and believe or not, but Popeye, Olive Oyle and Bluto, and even the postman pops out to see everyone.

You can go into all the houses and if you have seen the film, well you will recognise every one of them, so much so you expect to see Robin Williams as Popeye, walking down the street himself!

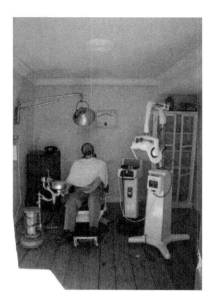

The entertainment is fantastic and the Animators, who play the parts, are full of energy and life. They sound like their characters and get everyone to stomp and clap along, and sometimes join with their dancing.

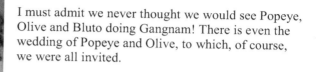

I must admit we never thought we would see Popeye, Olive and Bluto doing Gangnam! There is even the wedding of Popeye and Olive, to which, of course, we were all invited.

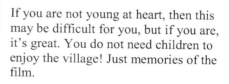

If you are not young at heart, then this may be difficult for you, but if you are, it's great. You do not need children to enjoy the village! Just memories of the film.

There is a silversmith working the intricate Maltese filigree in his shop. We stopped and watched him. Mike feeling slightly envious at the skill as, being a

creative person, he would have loved to have tried it. One day, perhaps.

One brief story. When we first arrived a cat came out, looked at us and disappeared, and we never gave it another thought. Until lunch time. After we had been in all the buildings, walked around the streets and generally had a good nose everywhere, including sending an email to Jacky from the post office, we decided there was no more to be seen and headed for the restaurant.

Off into the Seafarers rest for the most beautiful chicken and bacon carbonara. Whilst we were waiting for it, with the sun and the breeze, the magnificent views and the ambiance, we were joined by the cat and his mate. One sat on one side of Mike and the other sat on the other side, facing me. We thought little of it at the time, except it did cross our mind that other people had received their orders and the cats stayed next to us. And so we waited. The four of us, with Mike and I taking photos and videos of the scene and everything it had to offer. And boy, were those cats patient!

Our food turned up and the smell, the look in fact, everything about it was just gorgeous. And the cats had sat there for 15 minutes, not looking at anyone else's food, just sitting there.

We thought we would try something, after all we had a tremendous amount of food on our plates, so we each passed the cats down a piece of pasta, thinking, well cats don't eat pasta and so they will go away. Did they 'eck. They sat there happily loading up on everything we gave them. We have both had cats and never in our lives had we ever thought of giving them pasta to eat!

Other people seemed to be eating the obligatory burger and chips, so we can only presume that the cats did not like 'foreign' food and preferred local food, which is a mixture of Italian and Arabic.

By the time we left we had spent nearly 4 hours there, wandering around the village, talking to the Animators. In fact, Bluto brought down his pet rabbit for us to see as well!

We really did not want to leave, but we said we would return.

So onward and upwards to the Red Tower we went, having taken lots of photos and lots of video.

The rest of Saturday

We left Popeye's village with a heavy heart, but then we faced forward and wondered what else awaited us.

We drove slowly up the road, keeping away from the new one, and turned towards the top end of Malta, just following the road and our noses, then we saw the tower and turned off onto the rocky road that led up to it.

We parked up by a wall, got out of the car, stepped up through a gap and there was the northern end of Malta, Comino and Gozo laid out before us.

It was stunning!

In the distance we could see a fantastic palace of some sort on Gozo, and on Comino was yet another tower, as well as one of the far end to us on Malta. These towers were built by the Knights Templar when they lived on Malta as part of the fortification and if you went up one, you could see two more so a message could easily be passed right around the island if it were ever to be threatened.

Down below was a ferry service that a couple of cars were using, so we were pleased to see how we could get to Gozo if we went.

The wind was blowing hard, and the sky darkened over and we felt the first few drops of rain. Mike went to see if the tower was open but unfortunately it was not so we got into the car and headed back to Sliema, only the rain stopped within 10 minutes, and so did we as we came upon a beautiful view which we just had to get out and look at!

We pulled off the road and saw a large sign, telling us we were at ll-Majjistral Nature and History Park. From where we stood we could see an observation tower, however, as the weather seemed unable to settle we carried on back to Sliema, but on turning round we saw the whole open space behind us.

From our vantage point we could see that the land was divided up into small working farm areas.

We were in no hurry so Mike slowly drove along with the sea to our right and then we saw a sign we recognised and cut across to Il-Mellieha, driving past the same view we had seen not 5 minutes before. There were wonderful stone walls surrounding what appeared to be, large allotments or maybe small farms, all the way across to the outskirts of the town where we turned right and started the journey proper.

On the Friday we had discovered a supermarket up behind us in Sliema, so, once again keeping the sea to our left this time, we recognised various places, saw where the horse had been swimming, then a college or something, not sure what it was but managed to read the words 'Institute of Tourism, Travel and Culture', and with that came the memory of 'Olive' mentioning she was studying at an Institute for Tourism. So we concluded that this was it.

Very quickly we entered the built-up areas again, as during this time we had been going through countryside and small villages.

We went down a road we thought we had recognised, then turned left, only to find ourselves heading for the Hilton, and oh boy did we stand out from the Ferraris and Porche's etc, that were pulling up outside, so we carefully skirted the small roundabout to get out as unobtrusively as possible, though they could not fail to miss the tourists in the little car with their Australian cowboy hats as they drove past slowly!

Pulling out back onto the main street we saw the corner around which we knew was the car hire shop and turning down that way, we travelled along the sea front eventually reaching the area where Bubbles was. Pulling over to the right we headed for the supermarket, drove into the multi-storey car park, under the barrier and up, and up to the fourth floor before we could see somewhere to park.

Mike went to get a parking ticket and as he walked back, I noticed THAT look on his face. Wondering what was wrong I dared to ask him and he replied with, 'we need to get out of here....quick!'

As he pulled out of the parking bay and we started down the winding way out, he explained that the parking fees where UP TO €20 for the first 30 minutes! Nearly £20 to park for half an hour! Then 30 minutes to 1hr was up to €35!

We got to the barrier where, thankfully, there was an attendant who explained that we should have gone into another smaller area *below* on the right and then the parking would have been free, however, we played it safe, drove back out to the seafront and parked down close to the pavement running alongside the water's edge, next stop Italy, and walked back.

Now, shopping in the Tower Supermarket is slightly different to shopping at home in that some of the food, such as the bakery, is concessions who take the money for goods brought there and then.

If you should use the lift, do NOT buy the stuff right in front of it as you get out. We needed some shampoo and as we got out we saw it right in front of us. I could see nothing below €2.50 so asked a young man, who then led us to where the more convenient priced food was, on another shelving system.

It paid to look around!

We paid for our food, then carried it back to the car, got in and drove around along the coast, through a tunnel and onto The Strand, looking for a place to park as close to the hotel as possible.

Right on the doorstep on the opposite side of the road suited us fine!

We collected our key, as by now time was creeping on, and went upstairs, tired, happy, feeling free from the restraints of time keeping and with lots of adventures, photos and video to write about and post on here!

So Good night, sweet dreams and sleep well.

CHAPTER 6

Or

Never mention politics on Malta

Well, I can't believe it, we are up early again! And yet another wonderful sunrise coming up between The Strand and Valetta. The sun was just below the level of the sea, so I grabbed the camcorder and set it up, determined to take a reminder home of the glorious sunrises on Malta. Whilst the camera was running I happened to glance across to the boatyard to see horses being taken down for what appeared to be a paddle in the sea.....at 5.30 am!

After breakfasting on Maltese bread and boiled eggs, I packed a basket of ham, Maltese cheese and cold omelet and we popped over to see Greg and Caroline.

We had felt a little guilty about getting the car and not booking with them after all the information they had given us. We explained the reason we got the car, and they totally understood, after all, as they themselves said, there is not much fun clock watching!

They also realised, the same as us, that we were limited with the crutches as my walking was a little slower than others and getting up and down onto buses and sitting there in the heat when on the move was not going to be too pleasant either.

Mike, being the sort of person he is, went to shake hands with Greg, and left him some Euros to get a drink for himself and Caroline. Greg was somewhat taken aback, and, reaching over the top of the small shelf, handed Mike a couple of free tickets for a Grand Harbour Ride. He already knew we were going to stay in on Monday, during the election celebrations, however, as the boats were just up the road from the hotel, he suggested that would be the day to go on one as the celebrations probably would not start until midday. Mike thanked him and we left to head for the Tarxien Temples, a 16 minute drive according to Google.

We followed the road around to the end of The Strand, then turned left and got our first glimpse of the marina, and The Red Car Club. On the Marina was a boat called 'The Black Pearl', thinking 21st century we thought it was meant to be the one from Pirates of the Caribbean, but I could not remember a mention of it during my research.

The Red Car Club (our name for it) appeared to consist mainly of red Porsches, Ferraris and Lamborghini type vehicles. They were being driven by men in their late 40s, 50s, and 60s and followed each other round the island at speeds of which I am sure that if there had been a straight road from one end to the other would have seen them shooting off into the sea!

That was the last thing we remember about being on the way to a place 16 minutes away. The roads were horrendous.

I thought Sundays were meant to be a quiet day, not so this Sunday!

Some roads were cut off, and then we got stuck in one road where there must have been about 12 market stalls setting up, with red and white paraphernalia such as horns to blow and flags to wave.

One stall was having some beer delivered by articulated lorry, on pallets, being lifted off by crane. Neither of us had ever seen anything like it!

After squeezing between yet another lorry delivering beers to another stall, we started to make ground, only to be diverted yet again.

Police were obviously out, but not jumping on anyone. We thought there was a football game going on we did not know about! We carried on down some side street trying to find a name for it to go with the map, then some guy in a blue car went by, using his hands to say that we were talking too much and holding up the traffic. Funny, there was no traffic. It was a one-way street, and we had pulled over to let him past. Oh well, there is no pleasing some people!

Then we saw a landmark, the cemetery, and keeping it to our left kept heading towards Hal Tarxien. Which then disappeared, and we found ourselves in the middle of street after street of houses. There was no traffic, and we started to relax as we wound our way along the streets until we saw a sign for the Temple, which we followed, to the next sign, going up a street, which we followed, that led us to another street which ran the opposite way to the one we had just walked along.

We were not only totally confused, but very lost and, yep, you guessed it; the signs had disappeared!

Heading along a road, we suddenly broke out onto a slightly larger, busier road. So, turning left, we got to the end of it and found ourselves on a massive square, where there were crowds of men, no women, just men.

Going around the centre, we followed the traffic off the square and down a hill, saw a parking space, pulled over and took a big sigh. Our 16 minutes had turned into over an hour. Were we surprised? Not really, just hot, thirsty and frustrated, but not, I must say, unhappy.

Getting out of the car we headed back up the hill, noticing a massive building on our left, "bet that's the prison" Mike joked. "Er, if that's the police station then there is a good chance of it" I replied.

We carried on walking up and saw a policeman on our side of the road, smoking. Rather than interfere in his time off we headed for a group of men, outside a cafe, thinking we would get something to drink ourselves, but truth be told, we discovered it was a bar and already serving beer so, forgetting drinks but feeling brave, I asked one of the men the way to the temple.

Bless him, he was smiling away and told us how to get there, noticing my crutches he said it would be easier if we drove, we smiled back and said that it might be safer to walk with our track record.

We followed his instructions and, turning back onto the square, this time by foot though, which we later found out was the Piazza A De Paulo, crossed the road and walked up alongside the Paolo Parish Church, which we both thought we would have a closer look at on our way back.

In the beautiful sunshine we wound our way back through the streets, like the nice man had said, and then we saw the signs, again. We followed them, twisting and turning and then, oh joy of joys! A gateway leading to the Tarxien Temples! We went into a small house, paid our entry fee, was given a large A4 collection of information sheets all laminated and held together in the corner with a piece of string, to allow easy turning.

And so we entered the Tarxien Temples, our first true bit of Malta's history .Looking at the 1st sheet, we started to walk around.

The rocks were nothing more than monoliths in some cases. How they got there is like the same mystery as Stonehenge, and as we walked around, we realised it was quite a size.

We took our time; we were in no hurry, reading the cards as we went, walking on the wooden walkway that was about 6 feet above the ruins, giving a good unobstructed view and then leaning over the barrier and peering down into them.

There was hardly anyone there. The whole place was a suntrap, and it felt calm and ordered, until Mike dropped the guide over the edge of the railings. Looking around to see if there was anybody who could help, he decided to pick it up himself. He

walked back a little way, climbed through the barrier, down amongst the ruins, picked up the guide and then, in the true traditional way of a clutz, which he is not, that's my job, clouted his ankle on a metal strut as he climbed back up onto the walkway.

He went white as a sheet, stood up slowly and hobbled towards me. He said he was alright and so we continued, albeit slowly, around the temples.

It took us a whole hour to go around and we loved it, perhaps because at one point you actually get to walk amongst the temple remains themselves, giving you an idea of size and grandeur, of the struggle to build them, and of course the history, to feel it and touch it.

These temples were built 2500 years before Stonehenge! 2300 years before the first Pyramids, in fact they have been claimed as the first free-standing buildings in the world. But they are not the oldest in Malta!

We finished our tour and Mike was now hobbling so much I worried he may not be able to drive, so

we slowly make our way back to the car.

The streets were wonderful, people looked at the two strangers and we smiled back at them as we passed though the historical streets, lined with the houses with their Arab influences, it was amazing.

We actually found our way back to the car and, as we got in, I heard Mike yelp a little, but again he said he was ok.

We pulled away. And headed for Mdina. Well, that was the theory. According to Google, its 21 minutes away, but, once again, we got totally lost. Streets had been closed off for parties, police were redirecting, which is ok for locals, but what about us!

We ended up driving along a small narrow lane; it was lovely. We could see Mdina on the hillside in the distance, so knew we were heading in the right direction. We eventually pulled out onto the main road; the car climbed the hill, round a sharp bend and straight past the turning for Mdina. We drove on through the small surrounding town when  suddenly a lorry full of people with red and white flags, shouting, waving and using horns came round the corner and went straight past us. We decided to pull over at the next possible parking space as suddenly things had started to get noisy and scary.

 We rounded a corner and saw a car park, pulled in and Mike parked under a tree. All went quiet as we looked about us, only to find we had pulled up outside of a monastery, quick search through all our paperwork and we soon found it. It was a Dominican Monastery. The doors were open with a welcome sign just inside. We climbed out the car, through the doors, and entered an area of complete serenity. Inside was a courtyard, and in the centre of it was a grove. It was shaped in a square, with columns between us, and on the outer side through which we had entered, were the walls, thick walls.

We followed the square, hearing music from one source, then singing, then the smell of food. Meanwhile, I watched Mike seeing his first ever orange and lemon trees. The place looked familiar. There was something about it. We discovered later it had been in a couple of films and TV programmes, one being Game of Thrones. The silence was wonderful, and we fully appreciated it after the morning's hassles.

We wondered around for a while, and then headed back to the car to resume our drive back to Mdina, but this was not going to happen easily as the street we had to go down was now blocked with an accident between a bus and 2 cars. So we decided to follow the map. Yes, I know, we have been there before. Whilst we sat there we watched as some cars and lorries went by, covered in red and white flags, music on full blast shouting and clapping. We knew they could not get past the accident and appeared to be pulling off down a side street, something we did not want to risk as 'getting lost' seemed to be our mantra.

We headed out, following the road down towards the sea, we think!

About a mile down the road, having missed our turning yet again, we saw a man parked on the side selling fresh fruit and veg, so we pulled over.

Fresh figs, cherries for Mike, strawberries, what more could a person want?

We used the parking space to turn around and slowly made our way to Mdina, and yes, this time we got there!

We parked in the car park and, with Mike now on one of my crutches, me on the other, we made our way to the city of Mdina, only, before we got there I could see Mike was struggling, his face pale and definitely in pain. I went on in to see the layout of the land, so to speak, and he

followed me slowly. I told him it was a place with few steps and so we continued on our way, we went along one street and saw a coffee shop. It was obvious Mike was still not coping so we went in, ordered some coffee and a biscuit to eat. I was rummaging in my pockets when I found a painkiller, which I gave to Mike, he took it and, when we had finished our coffee, left the cafe and decided to go back to the hotel.

We headed to the exit of Mdina with the promise we would visit another day, then, whilst walking back to the car we noticed the Roman Villa.

That was it. The frustrated archaeologist in us both reared its head. This was something we had always wanted to see, and suddenly Mike was heading in that direction. I told him it could wait, but he said he wanted to achieve something today and he felt this would be it.

So in we went.

It was fantastic; the Domus Romanus (to give it its proper name) was something else. The pottery, the statues, the mosaic floors, and then we went outside. It was all amazing. And with walking slowly, then stopping, then walking slow again, and all

this time Mike did not limp, or complain about his ankle at all, seems like the painkiller had worked and so it was not long before Mike gave me back my crutch, and was happily snapping away as I filmed.

We signed the book and could not believe what people had written before us 'is that it?' 'Spose it was okay' just to mention two of the uneducated peoples' thoughts, obviously they have no soul! So we left our comment, showing that not everybody was ignorant to the beauty of the Roman Villa.

Phil had mentioned the lack of lizards as we excited the villa to which I said 'shush' and pointed just ahead of us, and there was his lizard, which he then spent the next 10 minutes photographing! A noise made the lizard disappear; it was a lorry, honking its horn, people shouting in the back, waving red and white flags.

We went back to the car park and decided that now was a good time to go back to the hotel as it seemed things were heating up on the roadways and we remembered seeing all the beer that was being put out so, thinking it wise to be safe than sorry we got back into the car and slowly headed back to Sliema.

I say we traveled back slowly because now the cars and lorries were building up, red and white flags everywhere. We came to the conclusion that the results must be coming in and that Labour appeared to be winning.

We followed the road down and then turned left just after Mdina. Further along we saw a signpost to the craft village and then we came to a roundabout we recognised, turned right and once again the sea was to our left.

We entered Paceville and, again, ended up outside the Hilton. We were getting used to this now, so just went round, came out and into the stream of traffic all going the same way as us.

The streets were crowded and what had taken us 20 minutes the day before now took nearly 2 hours just to get back to within a quarter of a mile of the hotel. We had been following lorries with loudspeakers on, people shouting and waving, and it seemed as if all the traffic was going the same way as us. How little we knew at this point!

The traffic was bumper to bumper on both lanes as we entered The Strand, and our only thought was to park as soon as we could. Every time I lifted my camera, people would wave and smile for me! Some would wave their flags as well! We were in the outside lane when I saw a free space coming up. We had stopped at this point, so on impulse I opened my car door and got out with my crutches. This attracted the attention of the people in the car next to us, and I asked if Mike could cut across and park. They were delighted to help, and kept their car still when they saw me hobbling after him. They held back so other cars could not pass and Mike pulled into the space; I got back into the car and we sat back and relaxed.

Then we felt hungry, so we emptied the car of everything, locked up, and hobbled our way to the hotel, worth the walk as we saw the cars and lorries with their flags and horns, loudspeakers and people all moving slowly along The Strand. We got to

the crossing outside the hotel where we crossed the road, and entered the hotel where we booked our tea, went to our room and headed straight for the window.

It was only 6'o'clock, and the noise had started. The traffic was mainly headed right to left we saw as we looked out of our room, with horns blaring and loud music from club sized speakers.

Meanwhile, Mike's ankle started to hurt again and before we went up for tea, I had a good look at it. There was one very nasty bruise on it!

Dinner was very different tonight, so many people were out at parties, the school children had gone and so we had plate service.

It was lovely. We had everything in the right order; the salad came first, then the tomato soup, homemade of course, then pork loins with vegetables and potato and then, surprise! Mike's new favourite, chocolate mousse, only this time served with jam pastries. I winked at the girl and she brought another one each. It is so good to see Mike eating so well after everything that had happened before Christmas!

We booked breakfast for the next morning and headed back to our room to see if we could sleep with all the noise going on outside. No problem, we were far too tired to stay awake and listen to the celebrating labour party, as that is who got in and it seemed like everyone under 30 was celebrating, as we had been told they would.

We finally discovered the reason for the rumpus around Sliema. Apparently the mayor is a conservative and the labour supporters wanted him to know that they had won!

So good night, sleep well and sweet dreams

CHAPTER 7

Or

Boats and more election celebrations

We got up early... again... set the video up on the balcony again and climbed back into bed; I guess with the hope of some more sleep!!

We dozed a little; while the sun rose, and the camera recorded another spectacular sunrise.

Remember, this is the scene that met us every morning during our stay!

One thing we noticed, as we lay there, was the silence.

All the noise had stopped at about eleven last night, and we got to sleep well after that, but today was going to be THE day, and if yesterday was anything to go by, we wondered if it could really be any worse! We had decided to eat breakfast in the hotel and so, about 8.30, we wondered off upstairs and boy what a setup for breakfast! Oh yes, we noticed that Mike's ankle appeared to have improved from the rest. The swelling had gone down, and he was walking a lot better, with barely a limp in site.

Muesli, cornflakes, different meats as well as sausages, yoghurt, beans, tomatoes, lettuce, 3 different types of bread for toast! Croissants, and some with chocolate too! Marmalade, 2 different types of jam, fresh fruit, grapefruit, peaches, apple juice, pineapple juice, orange and grapefruit juice, tea, coffee.

I could feel the calories piling on as I just looked at the feast before us. And once again, as much as you can eat! We felt spoiled! We tucked into our breakfast as we knew it was going to be a long day, also it was looking overcast outside so we

wrapped up well to make sure we would be warm and dry. After a good, but not too over indulging breakfast, we wondered back upstairs to get ready to go out. We checked all batteries were charged for all the cameras; we did not want to miss a

thing! Then we dressed warmly and wondered out into the streets.

It was not too busy and so we just meandered up towards where the boats were moored, found ours and we were the first on, so we got to sit at the front. It was drizzling slightly however we did not mind; we are used to rain coming from England!! Then it was time to set off and, rather strangely, as we left Sliema, it stopped drizzling!

The harbour is an incredible place of ancient and modern with opulence and wear and tear thrown in. Malta relies heavily on just about everything being imported so it has two massive harbours, one here and one down near Marsaslox.

This one though was just surrounded by ancient buildings, The Governor's palace could be seen at the back of Valletta, and then there were ships in the dockyards being worked on. The rich and famous use Malta as a

playground and some of the value of the yachts could quite easily feed a small country, I am sure of it!

The buildings, we recognised so many from films we have seen over the years.

Cutthroat Island and Gladiator are two that come to mind. The magnificent work of the Templar's was everywhere, in the walls, the buildings and the fortresses on the headlands.

It was just wonderful. Then after an hour it was all over and so we got back on land and headed slowly back to the hotel.

When we got back to Sliema, it was raining, again!

We headed back to the hotel, however, on the way we noticed a subtle change in the traffic, it was now busier, more flags, loud music, horns, shouting and waving. We were really glad we did not go out for the day!

Feeling damp, but not put out, we made our way to the rooms where we had hot showers, a basic lunch and then while Mike did some work on the PC, I read my Kindle.

In the background we noticed that the noise was getting louder, so we headed for the balcony to see bumper to bumper cars. Oh yes, and Labour had got in! Not only cars though, lorries, trucks, bikes, if it had tyres and an engine and could move, then it was there, covered in flags and full to the brim with people. The vehicles had hundreds of cans of beer on board and everyone was drinking; it was a little like Mardi gras with all the music and thump-thump-thump of the bass speakers.

We set up the cameras to record all these wonderful people. We had been chilling and now, in the afternoon, decided to be brave and go out on the streets. We did not go far, just to the corner where there was a café and had a cup of coffee each, sat back and watched the world go by.

It was not long before we waved at the people and smiling with them; it was certainly catching! The skies had cleared so instead of going straight back we crossed the road and, within minutes of being on the other side, Mike had found the anglers and of course, there was no stopping him then!! He sat and talked to them for about half an hour and they did not seem to mind sharing their knowledge of local fishing with him, especially when they realised he knew one end of a rod from the other.

Then it was time to head back to the hotel, make our way upstairs and then up to the restaurant for our evening meal.

Afterwards we returned to our room where we listened to the people celebrating again as they had last night, everything went quiet about 11 ish and we finally went to sleep.

Chapter 8

or

Could we really get lost that many times?

Yet another day dawned beautifully. We had only seen one day of the rain that had been forecast so decided we had been lucky in weather if nothing else. The holiday was going brilliantly, elections and all.

Today we intended to go to see where Gladiator was filmed, namely Fort Ricasoli.

Once again I got the directions sorted and off we went.

We followed the road from Sliema round the coast to Cospicua and, hopefully, Fort Ricasoli.

Thing is, we hit some road works which threw us off course, but we were used to this now, so we went with the flow, following the road all around the Grand Harbour, getting views of it every now and again, and just enjoying the marvelous sights of enormous lorries carrying what appeared to be stone up and down the rather narrow roads, and then we were back on route.

"Hooray" says I in my most confident voice, "I now know where we are again!"

Mike looked like he might believe me and continued to follow my directions.

"Okay, turn left, and then at the roundabout turn right" I directed.

We turn left; go down the road and......

"I cannot turn right, you have got us lost…again.." says my somewhat perturbed husband.

"No I haven't, look."

I show him the map and the street name, both on the map and on the wall of the street we have just turned down.

"Okay, I will give you that.. but why is there a market in the middle of the road?" says my now confused husband. *"Literally, in the middle of the road!"*

Now come on, if I knew the answer to that, I would truly know how to get us around Malta without getting lost. Wouldn't I?

We pull over and he decides we are going to have a mosey round. A sort of busman's holiday if you like. The market straddled the road all the way down and also off the turning to the right as well. We enjoyed ourselves with the sights and sounds, and the smells of the fish and vegetables in the hot sun.

It was very much like the markets we worked back home and similar to them this market also had many Chinese imports too.

I did, however, get myself a pair of long sleeved, half fingered gloves as I had been looking for a pair for ages to keep my hands warm and also to stop my crutches from making my hands sore.

The only difference we could see between this market and the ones at home was the amount of fresh food and the amount of choices we had, in fact, I do not remember seeing a burger bar there, something that is prevalent in the UK markets!

After a leisurely stroll we headed back to the car, looked at the map, then Mike, with the new information given by the navigator, started the engine did a U-turn and turned left at the top, after all, we could not get much more lost than what we already were!

But you know how the story goes, and once again we found ourselves, yep, lost. We decided to stop and ask the next person we saw if they could help us. Watching out, we suddenly noticed the lack of human beings. Typical!

We went down a dip, up the other side, and saw him, a gentleman strolling along. We pulled over; I wound my window down and asked if he spoke English, and yes he did! We both got a little excited and then asked him if he could tell us the way to Fort Ricasoli No problem, in fact it was on his way, so we looked at each other and asked if he would like a lift.

Without further ado, he jumped into the back of the car. No sorry, this large gentleman, about the same height as Mike but a little wider in girth, squeezed himself into our tiny car and introduced himself as Walter Perkins.

A very English name! He was a really nice guy, and we enjoyed talking to him. He asked us about our holiday and if we liked Malta. Of course we answered Yes! Then he asked us why Fort Ricasoli so we told him about how we liked to visit places where films are made, to which he stunned us by saying, "I was in Gladiator!"

Well, you know what it is like, people tell you they are in the film and you say "oh yes?"

"Yes, you will see me at 1hr. 46 minutes and 46 seconds."

Of course we had to get home and do the checking and low and behold, there he is!

We dropped him off, after getting details of where to go, waved goodbye and drove off to Fort Ricasoli. We worked out that having had information from a local nothing could go possibly wrong, could it?

We followed Walters's directions and eventually ended up outside the gates of Fort Ricasoli, that is, the locked gates of Fort Ricasoli. Mike got out the car and walked up to them, only to find a notice on the wall saying they are not open until May time and then only if

they are available to be open, by available we think it probably means no filming is taking place as the fort it a very popular place for filmmakers, for example *Gladiator* (2000), *Troy* (2004), *Assassin's Creed* (2016) and *Entebbe* (2018) as well as for TV in series such as *Julius Caesar* (2002), *Helen of Troy* (2003) and *Game of Thrones* (various). And all this from the biggest bastion fort on Malta, built by the Order of St John between 1670 and 1698.

Feeling disappointed, we took a deep breath, turned the car and slowly went back down the road. The sea on our left was magnificent, so was the Greek war boat, hang on, Greek war boat?

We were outside Sun Med Film Studios. One of the boats they used in Troy was sitting there on the beach. Amazing! We got out of the car and had a little wander around, but apart from the boats, there was not much of interest at that moment in time, got back into the car and had another look at the map and then we came to an executive decision...Valletta, the seat of power of the Knights of St John.

So once again we followed our noses, only this time there were plenty of signposts to follow!

It appears we made the right decision. Going towards Valletta was so much easier and before we knew it, we were there. Well, almost as we drove along the now 3 car wide carriage way with palms trees down the centre separating us from the oncoming traffic, we began to see another side of Malta. The house lining the streets appeared to be built of the same sandstone rock as the Tarxien Temples were, then in the distance we saw a monument and beyond that was Valletta.

We pulled up and found a car park fairly easily, it lined the road on our left and we could not really go any further other than to turn around and go back, so we parked up, climbed out of the car and started to walk up the main road, towards some incredible buildings which were behind a beautiful fountain, namely The Triton fountain. I think it might have something to do with the three tritons holding the massive basin in which the water spout for the fountain was merrily playing.

On the other side of the fountain was a horse-drawn buggy. We decided that if we had time perhaps a ride in one of those would be great, provided I could climb up into it. We carried on walking and came to the main entrance and thoroughfare to Valletta.

The streets were nice and wide and pedestrian only, brilliant, no jumping out of the way of cars, etc.

We meandered up what appeared to be the main central road, the buildings are fantastic, the architecture is a real mixture of very modern to very old, very Italian to very Arabian.. just a wonderful mixture of the culture that is Malta.

There are small alleyways leading off the main avenue that begged to be explored, but not today, another time, if we ever come back. When you consider that Valletta did not exist prior to 1552 and that before then all that stood on the peninsula was a lowly watchtower, which was then demolished for Fort St Elmo to be built at the far end looking over the water, and then one has to thank the planning, the labour skills and just sheer hard work of the men of the Order of St John and their Grand Master Jean de Vallette for whom the small but capital city of Malta was named for, and the money and assistance to build such a place came from all over Europe thanks to the increased fame of the Order.

We came across the Palace Armoury. Unfortunately, it was closed because of no electric. Ah well, Que sera sera. We wanderer on, through St Georges Square, where the water is divided up into lots of fountains that erupt on cue to music. It was lovely to see, and the children were running in and out of the waterspouts. We saw the end of the road, still some distance away, but decided to walk on anyway after resting on one of the many benches in the Square. The one thing I have not mentioned to date is that Valletta is a place to shop; big brand names line the road

as well as small traders with their wares. Thankfully, the beauty of the place overpowered all the modern retail goods.

We started on the last leg of the walk and, as we meandered along, we saw a silversmith and went in. He was working at his bench and we stood and watched for ages, and while Mike spoke to him about his craft, I wandered around. It was beautiful. The centre was a courtyard, bright and airy, and I just sat there and imagined what it must have been like to live there all those years ago. After Mike had his curiosity sated, we carried on and eventually came to the end of the walk, to discover St Elmos Fort. And what was parked outside? A buggy. After much deliberation, I think it was all of, "shall we?" "hell yes!" we agreed to take the buggy back to the square at the other end, namely where we started from.

I am so glad we have a sense of humour, and even the driver nearly wet himself with glee as Mike helped me into the buggy, using shoulder and hands and a lot of puffing and panting. But we made it. And what a lovely drive back it was, well worth the effort, and I didn't once think about how I was going to get out at the other end!

It wasn't so bad, just a little more huffing and puffing, the driver again nearly wetting himself, as were the other drivers, but the interesting thing was, as we laughed and heard them laughing we looked around and let them see that we were laughing with them as well, and they all smiled and said hello. We then had a treat, a piece of pizza which we took along the sidewalk, sat on a bench and enjoyed, before climbing back into the car, driving back to the hotel and made plans for our last day on this wonderful island.

CHAPTER 9

or

We meet someone famous and don't get lost

There is something that both Mike and I love doing, and that is fishing. Before we ever met, we spoke on the phone and he said jokingly, "I always swore that if I should ever marry again, it will only be to a woman who can put a maggot on a hook." And I had replied, "Never tried a maggot, I am a sea fisherwoman, I can put a live sand eel on, is that the same?" and since then our love for fishing has grown to include anything to do with fishing in any shape form or manner, teaching each other our different way. So on our last day we decided to visit the East side of Malta.

We decided to do a little history first, so off we went and yes, you guessed it; the roundabouts had us confused once again. We found ourselves next to the airport, then heading for Valletta, then back down to Marsaslox as we eventually found some sign posts. Travelling down the hill, where the scenery looked reminiscent of a desert, we saw the sign for Ghar Dalam, which is a cave where a lot of the history of the evolving of Malta has been found.

This place is fantastic. The history is amazing!

We parked up and, seeing there were no other cars, were a bit worried at first in case, once again, we were too early for the season. We got out of the car, walked through the door and the receptionist was there waiting. We paid, as you do, collected a map of the museum and then went in. The first thing you walk through is a museum showing the finds from Ghar Dalam itself, which is apparently under the museum, and there were bones!

Bones, bones everywhere! From the Pleistocene period they have found remnants of the dwarf hippo (*Hippopotamus melitensis*), the only dwarf hippo ever to be found and evolved on Malta possibly to the lack of nutritional food, the dwarf elephant, the giant dormouse, dwarf deer derived from the red deer, then the human intervention with pottery, flints, tools and ornaments. There are modern skeletons of the animals with the size, as they are today to give people a scale for comparison. For myself and Mike, it was a treasure trove. The amazing thing is that humans also lived there 10,000 years ago!

We did the museum and then, exiting at the back we very slowly, went down the slope to the cave.

Okay, Cheddar Gorge it is not, but it still has its own majesty.

Especially the bees.

As you approach the cave, you hear a gently humming and think nothing of it. Mike was ahead of me and entered the cave, walking further and further back. I could hear the humming all along the left, so I looked at the walls and saw thousands of small holes in them, from ground to ceiling, and bees flying in and out of them.

Apparently the bee hive in the rocks dates back thousands of years. There is a sign that says they are earth bees and are harmless, however, Mike is allergic to wasp

stings and that was a just a little worry as we all know, nature has a way of biting you on the bum when you are least expecting it. On our way back up we saw some school children sitting in the shade, having a hand on archaeological lesson. We looked at each other and we could see the jealousy of never having that sort of lesson in school mirrored in the others eyes.

We finally left to go back through the museum, got into the car and headed on down the hill to Marsaslox. We were rather excited as we heard they had a market there, well so we thought. As per usual there were a few wrong turnings and we ended up going through a small town called Birzebuga, where we stopped and asked directions from a nice lady who said that if we were interested in fish, we might also enjoy visiting St Julien Tower where there is an aquarium. Unfortunately it was closed.

We turned around and went to find our fishing village.

We found a little place to park up in one of the back streets and walked down to the front.

No market. Oh well. But the boats! The famous traditional Maltese fishing *Luzzu* with their colours! Each of them, with their eye painted on the front of the bow, purported to be from the Egyptians and Ancient Greeks, known as the Eye of Horus, which is said to protect fishermen whilst they are at sea.

I was standing there looking at them when I turned and saw an elderly gentleman sitting on a bench and just commented to him we were a little upset we missed watching them coming into harbour with their catch. And then we really started talking.

The gentleman's name was Frank Attard, and he turned out to be a famous photographer and then, even more amazing, he did an interview for us!

He told us about how he met and photographed the queen whenever she comes to the island.

A piece from The Times of Malta (which I discovered when I got home) sums up what a lovely man he is.

Photos and video footage are the only memories we have of the first visit by Queen Elizabeth II to Malta more than 60 years ago. Most of these photos were taken by Frank Attard, who has followed the Queen every time she came to Malta.

Frank Attard, who has been a photographer with the Times of Malta for more than 50 years, was present every time Queen Elizabeth II visited Malta – both on state visits as well as private ones.

Frank Attard says that out of the hundreds of photos he took of the Queen – his favourite is the one he took at Bighi where the Queen is seen with a woman wearing the traditional Maltese ghonnella.

"This photo with the ghonnella was also used by Malta Stamps," says Mr Attard.

The veteran photographer has continued to treasure every photo he has of the British Royal family – including that of the Queen's children, Prince Charles and Princess Anne, when they were young.

"This is the one I took at Delimara. Prince Charles and Princess Anne are playing in the sea with Lord Louis Mountbatten".

Frank Attard says that when he met Prince William last year during the 50th anniversary celebrations of Malta's independence, he had taken this photo of his father to show it to him.

"While I was speaking to him I took out an envelope with the photos of Prince Charles at the age of four, and Prince William was so pleased to see photos of his father at that age," says the photographer.

Frank Attard said that he has had many opportunities to speak with the Queen personally. He said that at certain occasions he was the only official photographer of the Queen.

"My photos would then be distributed to the other newspapers. Even British newspapers used to come and use our photos as they did not have permission to be at the event."

He describes the Queen as a very lovely woman, especially when she was in her prime.

"She was so friendly even when I went to Villa Guardamangia, where I went twice. I used to try and go to as many events as I could manage," said Frank Attard.

After the lovely chat we then walked along the front looking for fish. All we found was the small tourists market, so we went back to the car and drove up to St Juliens Aquarium only to discover it was closed.

We went back to the car and as we did not want to waste our last day; we decided on a trick we use in the UK when we want to go somewhere but not sure where, in other words, we followed our noses, this led us back to Mdina where we parked up and went to the dungeons. Oh, they were so creepy! Neither of us are into horror in any shape and these hit all the buttons, the wailing of the prisoners, the blood and gor, the means of torture that was being used on the dummies.. Oh.. Yeah.. Dummies, not real people, but at first glance you shake your head and do wonder! However, we had a great time as it really was most interesting!

We started to head for St Pauls, as we knew the way home by using this particular road, and saw a sign saying Ta'Qali, crafts village, so as we still had some time left we thought it might be a good place to see if there was anything to take home, such as genuine Maltese lace.

It is based on an old airfield and full of the old backed bean huts which have all been converted into shops and local craft shops. Although it was not fully open yet, we wandered around, looking at Maltese glass, Maltese stoneware and jewelry and even watched some being made, the glass that is. Although it was not all open, some of the craftsmen were there, adding to their stock, not a Chinese item in sight, everything being hand made there and then, and what wonderful craftsmanship!

Before we knew it, it was time to return to the hotel as the car was being collected at 6pm and we wanted to make sure we got back in time! We both felt somewhat sad, as the car was picked up and we had our last meal, packed out bags and set the alarm for 4 am.

Ah well, off to bed after a really exciting week.

CHAPTER 10

or

Do we really have to leave?

Once again we were up before the alarm went off, only this time it was to go home and not go away. This made us both feel gloomy. We sat in the dark on the verandah hoping to see the sun come up one last time, but knew we wouldn't as we drank our tea and ate the last of the food from the fridge, namely some toasted Maltese bread, butter and jam. Everything else that was not opened, we left for the staff if they wanted it. Mike and I had tidied the beds. He had slipped some euros under the pillow and our bags were ready by the door. Soon we were outside waiting for the minibus to pick us up to take us back to the airport.

We looked around with a feeling of sadness as we waited; we felt there had been a lot more to discover on the Mediterranean Island and we might never get the chance to come back again. The mini bus arrived, and we climbed in and as we reached the airport, we watched our last sunrise out of the windows. Now, as you may have guessed, if something could go wrong on this holiday, it did.

We headed to Ryan Air and booked in and Mike asked for our assistance, only to be told there was none available. All the assistance had been used up by others. I explained I had ordered it back before Christmas and they said yes, that's right, but whilst you were on Malta you canceled it. We asked for proof and they said I had phoned in. No, I had not, and neither had I been miraculously cured either! I was fuming. Unfortunately, when I get angry, I cry. We had not cancelled it at all. We had our thoughts and the only other person who had our information was the tour guide. Now, I am not blaming her totally, however; she was not happy that we booked nothing. I shall leave the rest to you to figure out.

I suggested I get on the plane first as I take steps very slowly; they said no, but they would try to do something. I felt awful because now I was a little old lady on crutches, crying, which made me cry even more at the embarrassment of it all, so Mike and I went and sat down while they sorted something out. Well, it was worth it. I got a lovely young man complete with wheel chair (one of the ones that had all been used up. We thought this interesting) to take me out to the van lift and eventually we were back in the skies.

The flight home had some amazing scenery, especially over the Alps. There was not a cloud in the sky from Malta to England and before we knew it we were landing back in Bristol, and climbing back into our own car and we headed home and it felt like we had brought the sun home with us as I spent the next few days sorting out our bags and doing the washing.

I looked at the bags as Mike put them under the bed, then we looked at each other and wondered wistfully if they would ever be used again for a holiday.

Thank you Jacky for such an incredible experience.

We hope you enjoyed reading about our first experience as tourists.

If you would like to see more then please go to our website.

This book has been taken from our weblog on www.firsttimetourists.com

On the site you will find many more pictures as well as videos.

Printed in Great Britain
by Amazon